Rescuing
Little
Roundhead

Rescuing Little Roundhead

SYL JONES

MILKWEED
EDITIONS

Names of some people and places in this book have been changed to protect both the innocent and guilty.

Published 1996 by Milkweed Editions
Printed in the United States of America
Cover design by Adrian Morgan, Red Letter Design
Cover painting by Fran Gregory
Interior design by Will Powers
The text of this book is set in ITC Giovanni.
96 97 98 99 00 5 4 3 2 1
First Edition

Milkweed Editions is a not-for-profit publisher. We gratefully acknowledge support from the Bush Foundation; Target Stores, Dayton's, and Mervyn's by the Dayton Hudson Foundation; Ecolab Foundation; General Mills Foundation; Honeywell Foundation; Jerome Foundation; The McKnight Foundation; Andrew W. Mellon Foundation; Kathy Stevens Dougherty and Michael E. Dougherty Fund of the Minneapolis Foundation; Minnesota State Arts Board through an appropriation by the Minnesota State Legislature; Challenge and Literature Programs of the National Endowment for the Arts; The Lawrence M. and Elizabeth Ann O'Shaughnessy Charitable Income Trust in honor of Lawrence M. O'Shaughnessy; Piper Jaffray Companies, Inc.; Ritz Foundation on behalf of Mr. and Mrs. E. J. Phelps Jr.; John and Beverly Rollwagen Fund of the Minneapolis Foundation; The St. Paul Companies, Inc.; Star Tribune/Cowles Media Foundation; Surdna Foundation; James R. Thorpe Foundation; U. S. West Foundation; Lila Wallace-Reader's Digest Literary Publishers Marketing Development Program, funded through a grant to the Council of Literary Magazines and Presses; and generous individuals.

Library of Congress Cataloging-in-Publication Data

Jones, Syl, 1951–
    Rescuing Little Roundhead / Syl Jones. — 1st ed.
        p.   cm.
    ISBN 1-57131-215-3 (alk. paper)
    1. Jones, Syl, 1951–   . 2. Journalists—United States—20th century—Biography.   3. Dramatists, American—20th century—Biography.   I. Title.
PN4874.J67A3   1996
070'.92—dc20
[B]   96-15052
                                                     CIP

This book is printed on acid-free paper.

*To my dear Father and Mother
and my four little roundheads*

Acknowledgements

The author wishes to thank the following individuals for their profound assistance in the difficult and still incomplete work of growing up:

The teachers and administrators of Columbian Elementary School in Cincinnati. The school building is now gone and so are many of the people who guided my often clumsy steps, but the memory of their generosity continues to warm me.

Walnut Hills High School for its insistence on excellence regardless of race, ethnicity, or social class, and its respect for critical thinking, creativity, and dissent.

Mr. Allan Howard of the *Cincinnati Enquirer*, who helped save my life by opening the door to professional journalism.

Augsburg College in Minneapolis, where professors John Mitchell, Lorraine Livingston, Barbara Andersen, Richard Sargent, "Doc" Olson, Ailene Cole, David Wood, Gene Skibbe, and others held my feet to the intellectual fire and encouraged me to pursue my dreams.

Russell Roth, my editor at *Modern Medicine* magazine, who would have enjoyed this book but did not live long enough to see it.

I would also like to express my heartfelt thanks to Mary Catherine Elizabeth Adams, wherever she may be; Rick Reckman and Sally Grad; Edward Tracy and Wayne Greenburg; Linda Sterling Goldman and Polly Nyberg; Burt Cohen and Dave Mona, two mentors who never knew that they were; Barry Goldstein of *Playboy* magazine; Jack Reuler of Mixed Blood Theater and Louis Bellamy of Penumbra Theater; and the many others whose love and generosity through the years has made it possible for me to write this book.

Finally, to my wife, Cindy, whose undying affection and encouragement helped me work my way through the darkness to whatever light this book may hold for others. She above all others knows that on occasion, I still need to be rescued.

Rescuing Little Roundhead

Introduction

The black ball swung from the crane, an enormous globe
pounding the wooden facade, sending shards of fiberboard
careening into the air, liberating dust particles the size of golf
balls. A small crowd of onlookers, some munching sandwiches, some drinking coffee, stood behind the fence, their
eyes riveted by the sight of such massive destruction.

In 1975, the city of Cincinnati, in the form of a few hard-
hatted men going about their business routinely, razed my
boyhood home in less than ten minutes with an iron ball.
There were no good-byes or speeches or commemorations of
any kind. When they had finished, the crew simply started
on the next house, and then the next house, and the house
after that, until the block that contained most of my childhood memories had been completely obliterated.

In the nine years since I had lived there, the combined
medical complex comprising Shriner's Burned Children's
Hospital, General Hospital, Jewish Hospital, Children's
Hospital—and a maze of underground tunnels connecting
all of these to the Hamilton County Morgue—had grown
exponentially. Some of the most important research in the
country had come out of these hospitals: both the Sabin
and Salk polio vaccines had been tested on children at
Columbian School. At Shriner's, severely burned children
were treated in hyperbaric chambers developed by NASA to
promote healing. My mother, a nurse for many years, had

been the first nursing employee hired by a progressive, crusading staff.

Our family watched "the Shrine" rise from the dust into a mighty hospital in less than two years. Since it was right across the street from our house, we saw the construction from start to finish. The big ivory-colored building carried with it a kind of benevolence and goodwill out of character for the neighborhood. But black parents often talked as if living in the tail end of Corryville made them upwardly mobile. After all, Corryville wasn't as decrepit as the West End or Over-the-Rhine, or even parts of South Avondale. When we first moved in, our next-door neighbor was white, and so were a number of other residents. But within a couple of years, the whites moved away and were replaced by struggling black families with two wage earners trying to keep up with the cost of house payments, insurance, and food and clothing for their children.

I saw clearly that the struggle to survive consumed these parents, including my own, so that their senses were dulled to the daily wickedness we children faced. Even today, my parents will say that we did not live in a ghetto, that it was a middle-class neighborhood where everyone had a job and nothing terrible ever happened. They are wrong. Something terrible happened to me on a day when they could not protect me, and that something has echoed throughout my life.

The economic stress and daily difficulties of these mostly Southern migrant families came down full force upon their children. While the parents worked or played bingo or chatted with each other across their chain-link fences, many of their children roamed the neighborhood in search of victims to vanquish, food to steal, fires to start. Fights were commonplace. The issue that hung in the air—who among us was the "baddest" — took on epic proportions in conflicts between older and younger children, boys and girls, kids with middle-class aspirations, and kids anchored to lower-class values. These conflicts shaped every single day of every year I lived in that house, and there was nothing I could do to alter that reality. I became a part of the conflict; the current of venom that ran through our streets like the raging floodwaters of the Ohio River swept me along with it.

As I watched my house fall to the ground, a chill came over me. This place had been alive with love and torment, a world of nurturing by a loving mother and punishment by a confused and angry father. Much that was good and all that was bad began here, in this house, which was finally being destroyed by an anonymous crew oblivious to the ghosts they helped to free, indifferent to the remembered cries and shouts of pain and joy that I heard as the ball and chain did its impersonal business. I had a powerful urge to help that crew pull the boards down, kick the doors in, break all the windows, set fire to the linoleum. Someone should have done it long ago — someone who knew its secrets and had the right to tear it down.

I would have been forced to restrain myself, had I actually been there. But I was not. I arrived in Cincinnati a few weeks too late to see the house come down. But I saw it all in my imagination a thousand times. I also heard the story from my mother, who worked across the street and saw the house blown apart from the force of the wrecking ball. From her I heard something that seemed incredible to me: my father wept as the last of the papier-mâché–thin walls caved in. There are stories aplenty in our neighborhood — there always have been. None of them, strictly speaking, is accurate. But all of them are true. This is just one of them.

Rescuing
Little
Roundhead

Family

The Beginning

It was December 1951. The little boy in his mother's womb was not due to appear for another three weeks. His parents waited anxiously because this child, like them, was colored, and colored people could not escape the ill-mannered, wretched, and sometimes just plain indifferent behavior of whites, no matter how hard they worked or tried to succeed. Colored people had to keep their mouths closed and their noses clean if they were to make it in this world. And task number one in the colored world was to teach every little newborn baby boy and girl the value of silence, of downcast eyes, of a cheerful grin.

In southern Ohio, such schooling could mean the difference between life and death. The Civil War had ended nearly a century earlier, but the ignorant hillbillies who ran the City of Seven Hills had never forgiven colored people for starting it. Had we simply been meek enough and followed the teachings of their gods, the Union never would have been ripped asunder, resulting in the bloodshed of 650,000 mostly white boys from the cornfields and forests of America, enriching the soil of Pennsylvania, Virginia, Tennessee, Kansas, and the Blue Grass State, to mention but a few.

At the middle of the twentieth century, the War Between the States remained a gaping wound to some. Cincinnati's legacy of abolitionist tendencies, beginning with the Lane Seminary students who, in the 1830s, took a courageous stand against mob rule, had largely been forgotten. The fact that the Queen City had once been Harriet Beecher Stowe's girlhood home and was reputed to be the birthplace of the Underground Railroad had also slipped from most people's memories. So much had happened to sour race relations in the intervening years that by 1951, Cincinnati had the vague feel of a city-state formed during Reconstruction, when the white man reasserted his domination and bands of roving rednecks rode through the countryside looking for a colored man—any colored man—to string up.

Fear deadened the eyes and ears of many a colored person in that city. Fear of what might happen should someone accuse a man of stealing, say, at Shillito's department store, or of making too much noise in a public place. White ears were sensitive to the loud guffaws of colored people, to the musical dialects of the day worker from Mississippi, the doorman from Arkansas, the ditch digger from Georgia. They were just being themselves, of course, but it took only one dirty look from the worst-dressed, poorest-spoken white cracker in the city to silence even a powerful colored man.

There is something about the ebb and flow of a river town that makes it seem both conservative and liberal at the same time, so it would be inaccurate to leave the impression that every colored person in Cincinnati was cowed by a few white ruffians in 1951. In fact, many who migrated there after the Second World War found the atmosphere more tolerant than in their hometowns south of the Mason-Dixon line. There had always been rich colored people in Cincinnati, colored people who bragged that they were Republicans, had money, were free before anybody else, knew the mayor's kinfolk socially, and were on good terms with the lads at the Friars Club. These were primarily light-skinned folks who had worked hard to assimilate the values of their Caucasian counterparts. In fact, they usually outdid them in being white and were often the first to condemn the Civil Rights movement as "moving too fast."

A coterie of courageous whites in Cincinnati had a family history of defying tradition and inviting colored folks into their homes. Some sought to help their more ignorant white brethren understand the struggle, and they did so knowing that their lives might literally be at risk. That they were genuinely interested in freedom and justice cannot be denied and gives the lie to the "white devil" theology still circulated by the Nation of Islam.

The little black boy came into a world defined by these regional and national histories, traditions, and peculiarities three weeks ahead of schedule, on a beautiful snow-lit night three days after Christmas, weighing only four pounds, thirteen ounces. Lord only knows why he was in such a hurry.

Mother

Mother called him her "little roundheaded baby boy," and the name stuck like a hickleburr. She put him on her slender hip and carried him up and down the stairs of the duplex they shared with Grandmama, Gran'daddy Willie, and Mr. Gene at 418 Elizabeth Street in the West End of Cincinnati. The streets were named after characters in the life of Jesus — Elizabeth, John, Mary, and so forth — and there were three churches within five blocks of the house. Grandmama's daddy had been a Methodist minister, a source of some pride in a neighborhood where the unrefined Baptists Gran'daddy Willie embraced dominated. The family went to the Methodist church only on occasion, sung those genteel hymns with controlled power and grace, then forgot what they learned in the sermon.

"Why don't you put that baby down so somebody else can hold him?" Grandmama teased her daughter. But Mother guarded the boy day and night, watching him with tender admiration, giving her heart to him through word and gesture. She searched his body for signs of malfeasance in the natural order and instead found perfection in every nook and cranny of the boy's being. He had a special smile and the look of an impish old soul that penetrated her heart.

He'd been born while Father was still in the army, but Father took leave and came as soon as he could. Nothing would stop him from claiming this child as his, for he was a boy, and he was the firstborn, and he was therefore a gift from somewhere—God, the Devil, somebody with the power to anoint. He saw his duty clearly: to make this child into something hard, like a piece of granite, so that he would survive the traumas implicit in colored life. He would mold this child with his own rough hands, as self-assured as a sculptor, as untutored as his own father had been, ready to preach the gospel of the leather belt.

Neighbors swore the boy never touched the ground in his first year of life. Mother held on to him as if he were a precious package. But at least once, she turned her back on him and something happened. The boy disappeared.

Gran'daddy Willie and Grandmama

The grin of a salesman and the temperament of a hotel doorman made Gran'daddy Willie mighty popular on Elizabeth Street. "Howdy do!" he said to everyone and no one in particular as he passed them on his way to and from work. A light-skinned black man with curly hair, he'd been a sign painter in the old days back in Georgia, when artists created their own designs, mounted a scaffold, and painted advertisements for Bromo-Seltzer, Ford automobiles, and Wheaties, the Breakfast of Champions.

Gran'daddy Willie had the knack of using just the right colors so that everybody in his paintings looked like they were about to come to life and crawl down from those signs. He knew how to space the letters so they could be read from a car going forty miles an hour down a dirt road or by a hobo in a cornfield. Gran'daddy Willie never talked much about it himself because he'd quit sign painting when the white man who hired him took him aside one day.

"I want you to teach what you do to these three boys here," said the man, pointing to three red-faced yahoos. Gran'daddy Willie hadn't been taught by anybody. He'd been given a gift and he'd used it accordingly. This Georgia cracker wanted him to give that gift to three gaping fools too ignorant or lazy to find their own talents. He knew that once he taught them, they still wouldn't be able to paint signs as well as he could. But the man intended to hire them anyway, throwing Gran'daddy Willie out of a job. It was 1938, and the Depression showed no signs of ending.

Gran'daddy's sly older brother Eddie had seen it coming and left sleepy little Newnan, Georgia, years earlier. Eddie settled in Cincinnati because it promised steady work, and he'd come back South a few times to brag about his new job at the Milling Machine company. "You need to get outta here, Willie, and come to Cincinnati, where a colored man can make a good living," Eddie told his brother. For a long time, Gran'daddy Willie let it go into one ear and out the other. He preferred the country life, and because he and Grandmama raised chickens and grew their own vegetables, the Depression hadn't broken their spirits. But when the man told him to give his gifts to those three white boys, Gran'daddy Willie put the past behind him and left for Cincinnati.

He'd come to this town of famous churches and restaurants to make a better life. When he arrived, he found he couldn't get into either the churches or the restaurants because he was colored, and that the better life he desired came at a steep price. The lights in the new house were gas, not electric, and Grandmama threw a fit. She had agreed to go north only because she expected the very best in household amenities. Gas was dangerous, but they simply had to settle for it. Shoehorned into a neighborhood with overcrowded brownstones, streets thick with young children playing marbles and mumblety-peg, numbers runners, and winos, Gran'daddy Willie found it too much to bear. He took to drink.

When he came home drunk, as he often did, Grandmama, the Queen of Disgusted Looks, gave him one for good measure. A pretty, high-yellow black woman with long hair and raised cheekbones from the Indian side of her heritage, Grandmama knew how to make a man feel like a penny waiting on change by shifting her eyes and mouth so that both of them narrowed at the same time. Or, if that didn't do it, she'd open her mouth in mock surprise and shake her head from side to side. Grandmama's Disgusted Looks could stop a fire truck.

This particular day, Grandmama didn't have time to give Gran'daddy Willie a Disgusted Look until it was too late. He came home early to "see about Sis," as he called his only daughter. Since the birth of the boy, Mother hadn't managed to put on any weight, and Grandmama and Gran'daddy Willie had been worried sick. Greens, black-eyed peas, corn bread, salmon croquets, juicy hamburgers, pork shoulder, rice with gravy—all these things Grandmama cooked to perfection. But Mother didn't have much of an appetite, except for once in a while, when she'd get a silver teaspoon, open the refrigerator door, and scrape ice off the inside of the freezer. She ate the ice like it was a snow cone, dreamily staring out the kitchen window into the tiny backyard.

The day Gran'daddy Willie came home early, Mother had left the boy asleep in his crib upstairs, away from the noise, underneath a ten-inch circular fan caked with dust and Three-In-One oil. Gran'daddy Willie came through the front door, looked around, called out, and heard no response. He tiptoed up the steps, his work shoes finding every creak in every stair. "Sis?" he called out again, innocently. No answer. He swooped into the room where the boy slept, scooped him up bare-chested and talcumed from head to toe, wrapped him in a blanket, and went down the back stairs tiptoeing and grinning all the way. On the way down he passed Mr. Gene's room.

"Willie?" Gene called as he caught the figure of his best friend out of the corner of his eye. Willie didn't say a word. He didn't want to wake the boy now that he'd managed to steal him. Just then, Mother, who had been standing by the back door eating ice scraps, took a notion to go to the front of the house. Did she hear her baby holler? Did she shudder as Gran'daddy Willie picked up her child and headed toward Central Avenue the back way? No one knows. Not even she remembers.

Gran'daddy Willie went through the alley across the street, holding the baby like a Ming vase, which he'd seen in old copies of *National Geographic*. The alley leading to Central streamed with people Willie knew, and along the way they'd holler to him, "Hey, what you got there, Willie?" Gran'daddy Willie stopped often and unwrapped his grand-baby, still fast asleep. "This here's my grandson!" he sang out with pride. And the old whiskey-drinking men in the alley suddenly became little kids again, competing with each other for a look at that baby boy. Had the child been a girl, they wouldn't have been so interested. Colored boys were special because they came into the world destined to be col-ored men, competing against the unfair rules established by white males — rules that prevented them from ever feeling like real men, unless they took special action.

Special action included learning how to find your way around the local saloon. So when the men in the alleyway finished coochie-cooing the boy, Gran'daddy Willie headed for the Courthouse Bar on Central Avenue. The air-conditioning ran full bore there, and the place overflowed with Gran'daddy's friends. He came in announcing, "This here's my grandson — drinks on the house!"

By this time, the boy had opened his eyes. He saw Gran'daddy Willie's smiling face, the familiar gold tooth in the front of his mouth, and what must have seemed like five hundred other faces pressed around him. What he smelled he could not identify, but it was strong and seemed to come from every direction.

Now, this boy never cried around strangers, and that day was no exception. He saw the bright lights and the colors of the pretty bottles and began to reach for one—not one in particular, any one—and the men all laughed at once. A couple of them tried to hand the boy their drinks, but Gran'daddy smacked them upside the head. "Get that damn stuff away from him!" he ordered. The barkeep got a rag and wiped off the bar as best he could so Gran'daddy Willie could lay the boy down where everyone could get a good look at him.

"Ain't he purty?" Gran'daddy Willie bragged. "Look just like his mama!" "Look at them feet!" somebody yelled. "The boy's pigeon-toed!" Gran'daddy said, "What's the matter with you? Don't you know all babies is pigeon-toed? If they wasn't, they couldn't never get outta the mama's belly—they feets would get stuck!" Everybody cackled at this, and some of the older, more drunken men nodded in solemn agreement. "He ain't got no meat on his bones!" another one protested. "Looka how skinny that boy is." Somebody else chimed in with the kind of quasi statistic heard only in bars. "They say beer'll grow hair on a man's chest—and put meat on his bones, too." "Give him a little Hudepohl beer, Willie! Ain't gonna hurt him none." A chorus of chums urged Gran'daddy Willie to make a man out of the boy right then and there. But, he had to consider the source: these were the kind of men who, if plain water touched their lips, would spit it out as if it were oil.

Gran'daddy called for quiet. "Shut up now, y'all—you scarin' the boy!" The tempest died down to a hushed roar. The boy played with his feet and chortled happily as if he were alone in the room. "Give me that there coaster," Gran'daddy Willie called to the barkeep, who slid it toward the baby. Gran'daddy Willie banged his hand down and stopped it just short of the infant. "He can't drink outta no bottle," said Gran'daddy Willie, frowning. He poured a few drops of beer onto the coaster and put it to the boy's lips.

That's when the wave of men parted like the Red Sea for the little woman in the no-waist dress, who fought her way to the bar and grabbed her baby boy before anyone could say word one. She weighed all of ninety pounds, stood five feet two inches tall, walked with her arms swinging in a determined fashion, and had a smile that would melt an igloo. Like her mother, she also had a collection of frowns that made grown men stare at their feet. She was wearing one of those when she snatched her baby boy up from that bar.

"But honey," Gran'daddy Willie protested, "I ain't doin' the boy no harm, honest!" Mother spun on her heels and addressed the crowd of boozers. "You oughta be ashamed of yourselves, every one of you! Specially you, Daddy!" The boy started to bawl on cue, as if to confirm his mother's judgment, and Gran'daddy Willie stood in stunned silence, utterly chagrined. Some of the men removed their hats when they first saw this fiery little lady come through the door. Others were just remembering to do so as she left. But Mother didn't notice. She took her baby boy home, talking a blue streak to herself, trying to hold back tears.

Father

Little Roundhead dearly loved the man in his life, the one whose eyes burned with determination, bitterness, and tough love. During the first two years of Little Roundhead's life, Father remained in the army at Fort Knox, visiting only on weekends. Fort Knox held all the gold in the nation in those days, but Roundhead's family saw none of it. While they lived in the same house as Grandmama, Gran'daddy Willie, and Mr. Gene, Father fought hard for control over his son. Grandmama and Mother seemed anxious to coddle the boy, but Father's intention was to expose Little Roundhead to trouble from day one as a way of teaching him to survive. Gran'daddy Willie and Mr. Gene had different ideas.

"You ain't s'posed to spank a child this young." Gran'daddy Willie spoke up one day when Little Roundhead was two years old.

"That's right," chirped Grandmama. "Let the boy alone. He's too young."

"Y'all wanna pamper this boy to death, and I ain't gonna have it," said Father firmly. "Spare the rod, spoil the child!"

"Who you quotin' Scripture to?" Grandmama growled. "My daddy was a preacher. You don't need to quote no Scriptures to me, mister! And I'll tell you another thing— Corinthians say 'Fathers, do not be irritating your chil'ren'! Maybe you didn't get that far in the Book!"

"Now, calm down, baby," Gran'daddy said. "What the boy do this time?" he asked.

"I don't care what he done. He's my son," Father said. "I can do with him what I want."

"Nobody disputin' that one bit," said Mr. Gene. "By rights, that's your son, and you can whip him if you want to. I got plenty of whippings when I was two years old!" Gene said cheerfully.

"Yeah, and look at you now!" said Grandmama, hands on hips.

"True 'nough," said Gene in mock remorse.

"Come on, boy—let's go home," Father said, picking up his son. "You gettin' mighty heavy." Of course he was.

Mother put two tablespoons of Karo syrup in every one of his bottles, and the boy had taken to formula like a robin takes to night crawlers.

Once they got upstairs, out of earshot of Gran'daddy and Grandmama and Mr. Gene, Father began to talk to the boy earnestly, like he was a drill sergeant in the army and his son was a new recruit.

"Look here, boy—look at me when I'm talkin'!" Little Roundhead didn't understand the words, but he felt the heat in his father's voice and sat up straight in his crib. "You lissen to yo' grandma, you ain't never gonna get nowhere. She think she know everything, but she don't. She spoiled yo' mama rotten and yo' Uncle Clay, too. Both of 'em wanna run the world. I'll not have it." He lit a cigarette and spoke as he exhaled. "When I call you, you better come, you understand me?" Roundhead didn't understand but he watched his father with curious brown eyes, following his every move as he paced the floor.

Mother worked from 11:00 at night to 7:00 in the morning, so Father took care of Roundhead until daylight. The boy listened as long as he could, watched Father pace in stocking feet until his infant eyes grew heavy, and fell fast asleep beneath the fan, the sound of Father's voice echoing in his dreams.

Mr. Gene

Officially, Mr. Gene was a boarder who paid Grandmama fifty dollars a month for a room and all the grits he could eat. Unofficially, he was a good friend of Gran'daddy Willie's, maybe his best friend, his drinking buddy, and his only confidant.

One night during the Second World War, Grandmama

looked outside her kitchen window while she was washing the last of the dishes and saw a hunched-over figure in the alleyway. She called Gran'daddy Willie to the window and asked him what it was. He said he didn't know for sure but it looked like a man leaning over a mattress. No sooner had he spoken the words than he strode out the back door to see what the man was doing. He took his pistol with him. Bad men had a way of finding the West End of Cincinnati, and if this was one of them, Gran'daddy would just as soon be prepared.

Snow had fallen the night before and the heat of the late winter sun had left the alley sloppy with slush that evening. Gran'daddy approached the man and found him trying to lug a semifrozen mattress down the alleyway. "Any trouble?" he asked.

The man turned, his glasses fogged over, liquor on his breath, and Gran'daddy recognized him as a casual drinking buddy from the tavern down the street. "Well, how you doin', Gene? What in the world—"

"No trouble," Gene said matter-of-factly. "My landlord throwed my bed out the window."

"What fer?" asked Gran'daddy. The man shook his head. "I don't know. Coulda been she didn't like the way I looked. Then again," he paused, "it coulda been she didn't like the gal I brung home with me t'other night."

"What you gonna do? Drag this mattress all over creation with you?" Gran'daddy chuckled.

"I might at that," said Gene. "I don't wanna trouble you none."

"You ain't troubling me none. I just feel sorry for you trying to lug that there wet mattress out here in this bad weather." It had begun to rain softly.

Gene stopped walking. "This and the clothes on my back is all I got till I can get in there and pack my things."

Gran'daddy thought a minute, then said, "Well, we got a room to let upstairs. Got a bed and a chest of drawers in it already. We was gonna see about lettin' it out, soon as we got it painted, but we ain't never got around to it. You know how to paint?"

Gene smiled shyly. "I don't wanna put you to no trouble, now."

"No trouble a'tall. Matter of fact, we could use the money. Fifty dollars a month is what we askin'. Can you pay some in advance?"

"Soon as I get my check tomorrow evening, I'll be glad to pay a month's rent," said Gene.

The two men went back to the house and had a cup of coffee and some homemade biscuits with butter and jam. Gene wasn't more than five feet seven inches, maybe 130 pounds, but he knew how to eat. Father used to say Mr. Gene had a tapeworm in his stomach, that's why he ate so much. Grandmama kept track of his vittles to see how much he really consumed. One day she told him he would either have to slow down on the Canadian bacon or fork over an extra two dollars a month. Pretty soon, Grandmama stopped buying Canadian bacon altogether. "I ain't got nothing against Canada," she said, "but they pigs is mighty expensive!"

When Little Roundhead began to crawl, he attempted to negotiate the stairway down to Grandmama's house because her presence warmed him. These excursions often ended in near tragedy as the boy tumbled down the stairs. From the top landing Father would laugh. "I told you to stay 'way from those stairs, didn't I? That's what you get for disobeying!"

Grandmama would pick the boy up and hold him tight. "Lord, this boy'll break his neck if y'all don't mind him up there." She took him into her kitchen, which steamed with fresh hominy grits, bacon, and cheese eggs. This is how Roundhead first met Mr. Gene—in the kitchen, his nearly bald head down, mouth open, shoveling in every last bit of eggs on his plate.

"This is Mr. Gene. Can't you say hi? This my grandson, Mr. Gene."

Gene brightened. "Hello, junior! How you today?"

"Shake Gene's hand, like a big boy," Grandmama commanded, and Little Roundhead put his hand out as he'd seen so many other people do. Gene shook it awkwardly, then went back to shoveling in the vittles.

Grandmama got out the phone books and sat them on a chair, after which she made a plate of cheese eggs and bacon, then put Little Roundhead on the phone books to raise his mouth to the level of the plate. The whole time, she talked baby talk to him: "You hongry, ain't you, sugar doll? Yeah, that's gradmama's baby! I know your daddy don't feed you up there. That's all right. You just come see your grandmama. I always have something real good for you!" She didn't have to tell him what to do once the food was on the table because, only a few minutes earlier, he had gone through the same ritual upstairs.

In effect, Little Roundhead had two families living in the same building. As he got older he used one against the other in order to get what he wanted. "Mama, can I go outside and shoot marbles with Junie?" "No, it's too late for you to be going outside," said Mother. "Can I at least go down to see Grandma?" "I don't care."

When Roundhead reached Grandmama, he simply re-peated the same routine. "Grandmama, can I go outside?" "I don't care—mind now, you just stay in front of the house!"

"Yes, ma'am!"

In those early days, after dinner, when the sun sat on the horizon like a big yellow beach ball, Mr. Gene would excuse himself and amble outside to the front stairs. He would watch the boys playing baseball, marbles, or football and tell stories of what it was like when he played, before the turn of the century. "I remember a time when we used a loaf of bread for a football. Rye bread—passes better," he would say, "and that was the onliest bread we had for two, three days." Soon the ballgame would stop so the children could listen to his stories.

"One time, we played baseball with a bunch of string I put together from my mama's dresses," Mr. Gene said, and while the children rolled their eyes and told him he was fib-bing, he added so many details they lost track of the truth.

"See, my mama's blue dress was her favorite dress in the world. Fact, she wore it to the colored presidential ball back when William Howard Taft was 'lected. But the dress had all these tatters on it, and Mama threw it in her sewin' bin so I just started to unraveling it and made it into a baseball."

"Didn't you get in trouble, Mr. Gene?" the boys asked.

Gene scratched his head, lifted his glasses from the bridge of his nose, wiped them with his baggy gabardine pants leg, and sighed. "Yeah—got the whippin' of my life, but it taught me something!"

"What it teach you?" the boys begged, wild-eyed. Then came the punch line.

"Taught me never to make a baseball outta women's clothes," he said. "You can't hit no ball made outta lace."

Then someone would ask the inevitable. "Mr. Gene, how old is you?"

"That's something don't nobody know," he would say, rising gingerly from his seat and shuffling back into the house.

"Betcha he's eighty years old," someone would say. Another might guess, "He's a hundred years old if he's a day!" One time, someone offered this observation: "If he don't know how old he is, he musta been born without a belly button," which made a certain kind of sense to the children.

But the truth was different. Eugene Cummins had been born in Fort Thomas, Kentucky, in the last century, probably before 1890. A fire at the courthouse had destroyed the birth records from 1809 forward, wiping out the crucial details about who was born out of wedlock and the exact relationship between the black side of the family and the white side, if there was one. Being an artist, and absent any absolute truths, Eugene Cummins played with the story of his life like it was a bass fiddle made to fit his fingers and his alone.

Picklehead

No sooner had Little Roundhead gotten used to being carried everywhere than along came Picklehead, his tiny baby sister. No one had said a word to him about changes around the house, but suddenly there she was—a little bundle with no hair and a pink blanket wrapped around her.

Little Roundhead pinched this adorable bundle to see if she'd holler. She didn't. He pulled her stringy hair to make her cry. She didn't. All she did was stare at him as if he were the newcomer.

Mother put the new baby in Little Roundhead's stroller and pushed her around the streets of the West End instead of him. He didn't like that, but he didn't know what to do about it. Also, Father came home for good when Picklehead was born. He picked the new bundle up and kissed it softly, mouthing sweet little sayings like "Daddy's girl!" and "Ain't you something—so pretty!" This was not like Father. He wasn't angry at Picklehead the way he was with Roundhead.

This behavior didn't make sense to the boy. Everybody wanted to coddle her, but Father didn't raise a fuss at all. Each time someone picked Little Roundhead up, Father made angry noises. What was the difference between the two of them?

Roundhead, old enough to speak a few words now, wanted to find out. Mother told him, "You touch the baby soft now—real soft."

"No!" shouted Roundhead. "Bang, bang!"

"No bang, bang," Mother corrected him. "You touch her soft, now—you hear?"

Roundhead edged up close to the pink bundle and laid his hand on her face softly, gently, stroking her cheeks. But something in him turned wicked, and in a flash he scratched the baby's face, digging his fingernails into her flesh and dragging them across her cheek. Mother, shocked and angry, grabbed Little Roundhead and spanked his butt.

"No! Look what you done!" she yelled, as she flung him aside to care for Picklehead.

Little Roundhead cried. But Picklehead never shed a tear. Mother made him go without supper—both upstairs and downstairs—as a punishment. He went to sleep that night confused and lost, like a vessel adrift on a river. From then on, he kept away from Picklehead while Mother and Father were around. But his awe at her silence prompted Roundhead to find ways to get Picklehead to respond. He finally succeeded on a Saturday morning.

Roundhead and Picklehead slept in the same room, with Picklehead in the family bassinet and Roundhead still in the crib. By this time, Roundhead knew how to vault over the side of the crib and touch down silently, so as not to wake anyone. He had learned this by trial and error, first by sliding out of the crib like a greased watermelon and tumbling to the floor, which woke everyone in the house, including Grandmama and Gran'daddy Willie. Then he tried squeezing through the bars and got his big head stuck between them, which made him cry. Father came out and laughed at him, said he wished he'd had a camera. They got him out by putting Vaseline all over his face and squeezing his big head backwards. "Bet you won't do that no more," Father chuckled.

Learning to get out of the crib without attracting attention took skill. This was a huge revelation for the boy, and he accomplished it as a result of his own single-mindedness. He was a schemer, a planner, a boy who rolled ideas around in his noggin until he was half crazed. He'd already begun to attack radios, alarm clocks, simple machines of all types, pulling them apart with his bare hands and staring at the contents. He never once put anything back together. This was why Mother and Father had placed everything that could be ripped apart on the higher shelves. Everything except Picklehead.

The little girl lay quietly, wide-eyed, on her back, content. Her brother slid out of his crib and found the flashlight Mother and Father left in the room in case the power went out. He padded to the foot of the bassinet and shined the light into Picklehead's face. She frowned. He reached up under the covers and found her big toe. He had noticed one day that the girl had fire beneath her toes and fingers. He wanted to free the flame burning underneath her big toenail. But no matter how hard he pulled, the fire wouldn't come.

Then he had an idea. He propped the flashlight inside the bassinet so he could get a better look. What he saw were tiny, light-chocolate-brown toes, perfectly formed, sticking out of her blanket, shaded by the deepest red color, the color of fire. Using both hands, he began to pick at her big toenail, pulling back parts of it that broke off in his fingers, forcing him to start again. He concentrated. If he could just get to the fire, he would know the secret of why Picklehead was so important to Mother and Father.

He got hold of a pair of pliers Father had left out, and he set about methodically clamping hold of her toenail and then ripping it away with all his might. In one yank, he exposed the quick of the nail and opened a large hole in the flesh that sent the fire—blood—flooding forth and Picklehead into a protracted screaming howl that so startled Little Roundhead he dropped the pliers and backed away. The howls turned into wails, and Little Roundhead went as fast as his tiny feet could carry him to the bathroom, where he retrieved a small bucket of water to put out the fire. When he returned, Father and Mother, looking sleepy and only partially dressed, were both bent over Picklehead.

"You do this, boy?" Father asked.

Roundhead nodded. "She got fire in her!"

Father knocked Roundhead across the room with one swipe of his arm, and the water bucket fell on top of him.

"I'm gonna have to take this girl to the hospital," said

Mother, since all they had at home in the way of treatment was Mercurochrome and Merthiolate.

Father got out the belt and Roundhead started to shed big tears, knowing what was coming next. He felt a sickness creeping over him, from his head to his knees, as he lay on his bed, waiting for the whipping. Then Father burst through the door like a wild animal and laid the strap onto Roundhead's backside dozens of times. As Father whipped Little Roundhead, he yelled at him about growing up to be a "responsible human being." It was the yelling and the screaming that caused the terror, even more than the belt.

When it was over and Father left him to lie there weeping, Roundhead buried his face beneath the pillow, shutting out the light from the yawning sun. It was only ten o'clock in the morning, and he'd already been licked.

Finding His Face

Roundhead woke whimpering, the salty tears now dried. He'd done something so wrong it could never be made right—he'd pulled his sister's toenail off—and Father had beaten him with the belt until he'd nearly passed out. He sat up, rejoicing: it had only been a dream! Why had he dreamt such a thing? Why had it seemed so real? He listened carefully and heard nothing, as if it were the middle of the night and he had been awakened by his own thoughts.

He tried to move, but the pain in his buttocks stopped him. He put his hand there and felt the welts from the belt and buried his head in his pillow again. What had happened came flooding back to him with agonizing clarity: it was no dream. The fire had been meant to stay inside Picklehead's toes, and he'd set it free, only to hurt her and be hurt himself. He hadn't meant to cause her pain—not like that, not in that screaming sort of way. He'd only meant to discover her special secret.

The experiment had gone awry. In the darkness, he listened for Picklehead's soft breathing and heard none. His tired eyes, weary from crying, met the gloom in the room. He gave in to it and lay panting, thinking, *What have I done? Why did I do it? Because I am bad. I am bad because I have done this.* He repeated the mantra in his mind, seeing himself perform the horrible deed again and again, each time trying harder to resist but never winning, never stopping short of the objective to *get the fire out!*

He had to pee. To pee, he had to get up. To get up, he had to move his legs. To move his legs, he would have to grow new ones. He was going nowhere except back to miserable sleep, condemned to relive his error over and over without forgiveness. Later, inside the nightmare, searching for a toilet, he found one just his size and let loose his distended bladder.

He wet the bed, soaking the mattress, the sheets, even one of his pillows. Roundhead felt deeply ashamed and got up quickly to change the bed before Mother or Father discovered his mistake.

In the bathroom, he reached for new sheets from the cupboard and pulled some down on top of his head, along with a pink hot water bottle and the spare iron. He knew he'd be punished yet again for meddling where he had no business being, but he had a plan: he would change the bed, scurry down the back stairs, and hang the offending sheets out to dry. No one would ever notice the difference.

The colossal noise of the iron banging against the

bathroom floor might have alarmed the household, but when Roundhead strained to hear, only the sound of muffled laughter came from downstairs. Men's voices, mostly. He felt a thickening lump beginning to rise on his head, throbbing along with his pulse, which sent him to the mirror.

Too short to stand on the floor and see his own image, he piled the sheets and blankets up, stood on top of them, and tried to peer into the glass. Still no sign of his face. He must not be high enough, he thought, climbing down to get more blankets. When he couldn't find any, he took a chair from the room where he slept, stacked pillows on it, then climbed up to see who he was.

There in the wobbly antique handblown glass he saw a face with a wry, ironic smile and brown eyes that twinkled as if they contained a bit of the sun or stars or moondust. The boy in the mirror had well-defined, happy features. The boy looking at himself had a lump on his forehead and knew nothing else—whether he was dark for a colored boy, the relative size of his nose in proportion to his oversized head, or where his mouth had been set in relation to his eyes and ears.

Roundhead raised his right hand to his face slowly, slowly, to be sure the hand that appeared in the mirror was his own. He touched his eyebrows and long eyelashes, brushing them lightly with his fingertips. He tweaked his nose and chuckled to himself. This boy in the mirror with the wonderful eyes and expressive mouth—this was him! Or rather, *he* was that boy. He smiled, winked, made funny faces, all the time controlling what he did to be sure he had the power to make the mirror be him. And he did. Through the mirror he became a real boy and could see and accept the person he truly was, inside and out.

He had done a stupid thing to Picklehead. But when he looked at himself in the mirror and saw that he wasn't a good-for-nothing boy but just a child with smooth chocolate-brown skin and a big, passionate smile, he felt better. Just then, Father burst into the bathroom. Roundhead panicked. "I was just tryin' to change the sheets," he said.

Father gently took him down from the chair. "You wet the bed again?" Roundhead hesitated, expecting a swat on the behind. Instead, Father rubbed his head and smiled. "I'll take care of that. You go down and say hi to your Grandmama. She's been worried about you."

Roundhead scurried downstairs in his underwear. All had been forgiven and the guilt had been lifted from his shoulders.

"Well, you some kind of rascal, ain't you, pulling your sister's toenail off? I declare!"

"Didn't mean to, Grandmama."

She reached out to Little Roundhead. "Come give your grandmama some sugar."

Gratefully, the little boy ran into Grandmama's open arms. She kissed him and hugged him tightly. "That's all right," she said. "Anybody can make a mistake," and she squeezed him so long and hard he began to feel that something might be wrong. But soon she let him go and said with a grin, "How 'bout some cheese eggs?"

To Goodman Street

Elizabeth Street

Inside the house at 418 Elizabeth Street, conflict raged around child-rearing practices and attitudes about pain and suffering. It seemed to Roundhead that the old Southern part of the family—represented by Grandmama, Gran'daddy Willie, and even Mr. Gene—wanted little more than peace and quiet. Often Little Roundhead heard Grandmama mutter, "I can't get me a minute's peace!"

Instead, there was confusion, chaos. People spoke to each other sharply while feigning civility. Roundhead quietly observed that adults seemed to know how to do things but not how to talk about them. "Let's not fight in front of the babies," became standard language, but by now Roundhead and Picklehead were used to hearing shouts and sometimes curses from members of the family.

During these conflicts, Roundhead usually clung to Father. Father was the only one who seemed to know what he wanted, and he had a hard outer shell that protected him from the blues, that queasy feeling of misery that crept through the house. Mother got the blues more than anyone else, and when she did, she hung around Grandmama to talk about it in the high-pitched, determined voice that often marks the speech of Southern black women. This music first awoke in the boy his own instrument, an instrument that superseded his mind. Something in the voice sprung from the heart and spirit of the self. He loved to cock his ear and listen:

"You say you gonna do what? Don't you be lettin' them peoples push you around now like you some kinda broom, 'cause they sho' 'nough will try you," said Grandmama.

"I don't know what I'm gonna do about it, but you can believe you me something will be done!" said Mother.

"Well, all right! Just 'cause you colored, now—"

"That's no reason!"

"That's what I'm sayin'. You gotta show them folks they have no chance of runnin' over you, not one chance!"

Talk like that went on for days sometimes, a round-robin of grievances, struggles against hypocrisy, blatant discrimination—things Little Roundhead only vaguely understood. Years before, Mother had to quit Bennett College in Greensboro, North Carolina, after only two semesters because Grandmama got arthritis in her back and legs and could barely walk. Without enough money to continue her schooling, Mother came home, nursed Grandmama back to health, and eventually joined the army. There she excelled at accounting and something called routineering, and she was prepared to go to work at Procter & Gamble. But even after the woman at the company said her test scores were very high, she never called Mother back.

Shocked that she could have fallen victim to such a common and indefensible mind-set—the assumption of colored inferiority—Mother spent weeks talking to her family about the experience. She had been sheltered by her light skin and gracious manner against many of the experiences of other black women. There were times when white people didn't know she was a Negro, but she never tried to hide her race.

She had been forewarned that her ultimate goal of

becoming a registered nurse would lead to disappointment, because the nursing schools allowed only one or two blacks into their programs each year. Still, she doggedly applied, only to be turned down. Finally, she was forced to lower her sights and take a more humble position as a licensed practical nurse, who could do procedures and administer care but couldn't "pass medicines." Mother's motto, "Nothing beats a failure but a try," served her well during those dark days of struggle.

According to family legend, Little Roundhead was four years old the first time he committed an act of public violence. Grandmama had thoughtfully given him a Tonto outfit on his fourth birthday, which he wore as he watched episodes of *The Lone Ranger*. Tonto, invariably beaten savagely each week by the bad guys, said very little to protest this treatment. On one particular occasion, Grandmama had been especially vocal in urging Roundhead to help Tonto.

"Save him! Save Tonto!" she cried with mock excitement. Forsaking the rubber tomahawk that came with the cheesy outfit, Little Roundhead toddled off to the hall closet and returned with a real hammer so big he could barely hold it with two hands. As Tonto dutifully took blow after blow from the bad guys, murmuring "Where Kimosabe?," Roundhead let out a war whoop and charged the old Philco, smashing the screen dead center, cracking it in several places.

"Ohhhh, Lord! Look what that boy done done to my TV!" Grandmama shouted as she jumped up, eyes big as serving platters. "What you go do a fool thing like that for, boy?" she screamed.

Little Roundhead clung to Father's pants leg and mumbled, "You said to help Tonto, Grandmama!"

Father's laughter shook the boy's grip. "I warned you not to be agitating the boy like that. C'mon son—let's go home. And I ain't about to pay for that TV, neither!"

Grandmama was part Indian, which is why she proudly gave Roundhead a Tonto outfit instead of the standard Lone Ranger getup that all the other boys had. Roundhead was the only kid in his neighborhood with an Indian costume. When it came time to play cowboys and Indians, he had to be the Indian. This set a comic pattern for the rest of his life: he would often find himself the underdog, struggling against the status quo.

Father found a new home for his family just in time. Little Roundhead grew more impish every day and Grandmama had tired of his antics. But Father relished the times Roundhead tested Grandmama's nerves, like the day he took grease pencils and created a mural on her newly painted walls. The grease pencils had been a gift to Roundhead from Gran'daddy Willie, who thought he saw something of the artist in the boy. Father had remarked, "That boy ain't gonna do nothing but mark all over your walls with them pencils," to which Grandmama had scoffingly replied, "You always trying to keep the boy from expressin' hisself."

When Roundhead completed his mural on the lower part of the living-room wall, he hurried to get Grandmama so she could see it. Grandmama hustled into the living room with a smile on her face, then burst into tears, shouting, "Oh, Lord—no, no, no, no, no!" She had to steady herself with one hand on the rocking chair while she wiped her eyes and yelled, "Look at what you done did to my wall, boy! I'ma tear your little butt up!"

It would not be the last time a critic objected to Little Roundhead's art, and one could argue that Grandmama's spanking was a fitting way to begin an artistic career. Like most young artists, Roundhead thought the mere fact that he had done something, anything at all, was positive.

Moving Away

The new house at 225 Goodman Street, in the midst of what had been a largely white middle-class neighborhood as late as immediately after the Second World War, had six rooms. The living room led to the dining room, a room that had the pretension of French doors that opened to the kitchen. Upstairs were other rooms that Mother and Father rented to people who came and went at all hours of the day and night by a separate door on the side of the house. The door between the upstairs and downstairs stayed locked for several months, and the family slept in the living room.

To Roundhead and Picklehead, who'd been used to having the run of a large brownstone, 225 Goodman Street was a step backward. The cellar contained dozens of old beer bottles, along with vats of DDT insecticide, whose smell permeated the basement and sometimes the kitchen upstairs. When Roundhead's family moved in, the cellar also housed several rat families. Until then, Roundhead had never seen a rat.

The side yard contained odd-sized, jumbled pieces of wood with rusty nails in them, concrete blocks, screws, ripped and torn mesh-wire screens left over from some truncated remodeling plan. Pop and beer bottles lay on the patches of grass inside the bushes surrounding the house. Roundhead soon learned that nearby stores would pay him five cents for each unbroken beer bottle, two cents for each pop bottle. On days when he had no money, Roundhead took off on an excursion around the community, looking for empty bottles. At times, he found bags of them stuffed in trash cans. Twenty cents worth of bottles translated into forty gigantic baseball cookies at the Little Store, or forty cherry candies at Gebhardt's Grocery. He felt blessed to live in such a neighborhood, where cash money seemed to grow if not on trees, at least in the shrubs.

One day, while Roundhead snooped for bottles in the forest, the tree-lined area nearest the recreation center, he stumbled upon a large cardboard box, partially buried in the ground, covered over by pine needles and leaves. He'd seen it because he'd dared to leave the path in the true pioneering spirit, knowing that real discovery required some risk. A large chalky white rock sitting atop some oak leaves caught his eye. Roundhead stopped to listen, like an animal, and to sniff the air. The chirping of the birds and the scurrying of chipmunks was all he could hear, but there were no signs of humans. He looked in every direction and saw pine and oak trees that no doubt covered the entire neighborhood a century earlier, before the rich white folks had moved out to the hinterlands. He examined the rock closely to see if there were booby traps, wires, strings, or other things that could hurt him. He learned to do this by watching *The Cisco Kid*.

Roundhead kicked at the rock, pried at it with his toe, and soon found the cardboard box. Quickly, he lifted the box, or tried to, but it weighed far too much. He opened the top and found a cache of beautifully cleaned beer and pop bottles What good fortune! Roundhead had found buried treasure, every child's dream. These bottles would allow him to have his own spending money every day. All he'd have to do was redeem them a few at a time.

As he marveled at the booty and dreamed of extra cookies

and candies, someone jumped him from behind and wrapped massive arms around his neck.

"What the hell you doin' here?" asked a booming voice. "These my bottles!" The owner of the voice flipped Little Roundhead down on his back, pinning him to the ground. "I should kill you now," the massive black boy said. "But I'ma let you go this time. You better never come back here, though. Or I'll kill you for sho'!"

He stood up and let the terrified Little Roundhead run away. The boy, he later learned, was a behemoth named David Sawyer—at least three hundred pounds, six feet tall, and only in the fifth grade.

Roundhead had many encounters like this one with children he didn't know and had nothing against. The family had journeyed from the heart of the city into what seemed like the country, only to find that this neighborhood contained more strange and threatening elements than the city did. In point of fact, the house sat at the far end of an inner-city suburb rapidly on its way to becoming an all-black ghetto. The old white woman who lived next door moved out as quickly as she could when Roundhead's family moved in.

On the other side of their house, a wooden, three-story apartment building loomed, crammed with families who didn't seem to have fathers and whose mothers worked hard to take care of their children and also make a living. Next to the apartment house was an impressive stone facade behind which a man named Mel appeared to be raising a family of five children by himself. Roundhead's family didn't go out of their way to get to know these people, or anyone else going up the Goodman Street hill toward the big street, Burnet Avenue, where the buses ran.

Down the street, toward white Corryville, was an entirely different world. Roundhead's next door neighbor in that direction was Clifford Longmire, whose family moved in after the old white woman's son came to take her away. Next to Clifford's house lived the rowdiest brothers in the neighborhood in a house where vines, trees, and "wild thangs" grew. Darryl and Chuckie, two Southern boys known for eating lard sandwiches spread with sugar, seemed to live by themselves. A mother existed but showed up only at odd times. A father might have been there too, but if so, he kept to himself.

The alleyway that ran from Goodman Street back to Piedmont Street behind Darryl and Chuckie's house provided a convenient shortcut that led directly to the recreation center's doors and to important stores: Gebhardt's Grocery, the Little Store, White Villa, the deli on Highland. To get to the alleyway, any self-respecting boy would simply hop over the Longmires' fence, jump into Darryl and Chuckie's yard, crawl over the roof of an unknown garage, and tumble down onto the cinder-covered concrete. In the beginning, Little Roundhead made this strange expedition to escape marauding bands of boys.

But Darryl and Chuckie's yard overflowed with special challenges. The apple and peach trees and grape vineyards carried a certain kind of prestige in the neighborhood. Come harvest time, Darryl and Chuckie's mother generously offered everyone the opportunity to pick their own fruit. But after two or three years of neglect, as the trees shed their fruit and it burst open and lay rotting on the ground, yellow jackets, sugar bees, flies, gnats, and nits staked their claim to the air just above the yard, while rats, raccoons, and, some said, snakes lived on the ground. Darryl and Chuckie's yard became a kind of living science exhibit to be studied only by the brave, the fearless, and the supercurious.

The most important feature of Little Roundhead's new neighborhood had to be the ancient General Hospital receiving ward and grounds. Established sometime in the nineteenth century, the receiving ward connected underground to an amazing complex of hospitals. In the midst of this complex, the Hamilton County Morgue loomed, just a short bike ride from Roundhead's house.

General Hospital never closed, and the wailing ambulances speeding down Goodman Street often caused the children to plug their ears as they played their favorite games—hopscotch, jump rope, rock teacher, and marbles. The rec center three blocks away had the space and equipment for baseball, foursquare, tetherball, horseshoes, and basketball. An old tennis court sans net, covered with glass and debris, served as a setting for bike wars. Apparently, no one in Corryville knew how to play tennis in the 1950s.

From the first moment he arrived, Little Roundhead looked longingly at the large, rising retaining wall of General Hospital, which ran the entire block and continued down Eden Avenue toward the hospital's steam plant. He badly wanted to climb the wall, to prove himself master over his environment, but it was at least two years before his parents gave him permission to do so.

The roaring, screaming ambulances frightened Roundhead mostly because he thought they sounded like wild beasts. Police cars cruised the street, some delivering wounded criminals to General Hospital, others looking for crimes in progress. The police were omnipresent, which kept crime to a minimum in Corryville. But the cruelty index among the children soared as the years went by, and parents discovered they had yet to find the Promised Land.

Rats and Thangs

There was no basement as such at 225 Goodman Street. To get to the furnace, the washing machine, and the fuse boxes, you had to go out the back door, open the heavy wooden double cellar doors, and descend into a cold, putrid-smelling room with low-hanging electrical wires and water dripping from the overhead pipes. A medieval-looking furnace with eight outstretched arms occupied a third of the floor space.

In the daytime, Little Roundhead could manage to change the fuse by himself. But as evening came, the rats who tunnelled into the walls and ate away the fresh concrete ventured out to play. The cellar was their den, and they ran about as if they owned it. Who was Little Roundhead to argue?

During the course of several days, he and Father used a wheelbarrow to cart away the beer bottles and the DDT. Father decided to bury them in a pit at the end of the yard near the back fence. Roundhead helped dig the pit and enjoyed smashing the bottles, too dirty to redeem for money, against each other, watching them break into shards of glass, after which they were covered up with dirt. Father decided he wanted to cultivate grass there later, but nothing ever grew in that spot, no matter what kind of seed he spread. Inadvertently, Father had created a toxic waste dump in the backyard. To complicate matters, he built a sandbox, which became a playground for Roundhead and Picklehead, directly on top of it.

The first time Little Roundhead saw a rat, it was late in the evening as he walked up the front steps. At the top, he thought he heard a rustling sound in the bushes below. Little Roundhead turned and saw a gray furry creature, hump-backed, with a long tail, twisting and turning its way through a very small hole underneath the neighbor's fence. That had to hurt, Roundhead thought, because the tines of the fence had poked the animal, but nothing seemed to slow it down. It was the size of a small cat but, he thought, it must have the spirit of a snake or a lizard.

Soon afterward, he had to take the trash outside and empty it into one of three garbage cans. Before Roundhead could even approach the cans, the rats began to scatter every which way. Roundhead dropped the trash and ran back into the house. "Mama!" he cried. "Something's in the garbage cans outside!" Mother came to the back door. "Probably nothing but a rat," she said casually. "They're just as scared of you as you are of them. Go on. They're probably gone by now."

Summoning his courage, Little Roundhead took a deep breath and cautiously approached the cans, step by step, eyes wide open, ears tuned for any sound that would suggest the evil rodents were back. He reached the cans, dumped the garbage, and ran back inside the house, relieved that it was over. Until the next night.

Father tried to fight the rats, but the battle had been lost years ago. He put down poison, little salt water taffy-like candies, and it worked very well, except that the rats ate the poison and then crawled into the cellar walls and floor to die. Within a few days, the stench would reach clear into the living room. Father would take Little Roundhead with him to collect the rat carcasses that remained exposed, and to dig into the walls to unearth the rotted rat bodies.

On cold nights when a fuse blew or the furnace went out and Father wasn't home, Mother would put on her coat and say, "C'mon—we got to change this fuse!" Together Roundhead and Mother would brave the wintry, icy weather, open the cellar door, and wait—just wait for the awful scurrying to begin.

At other times, Roundhead would creep behind Mother, holding a worthless broom while she clutched a shovel and a flashlight. Occasionally a rat would crawl from behind a brick, sick from the poison but not quite dead, hissing at the two of them. Then Mother would raise that shovel and hammer the critter into the hereafter, using all her weight and determination. Roundhead would have to sweep the rat into the shovel, and Mother would dispose of it in a double-wrapped paper bag.

Such hazards haunted Roundhead's dreams. Father told them once that he had found a rat in the downstairs bathroom, next to the kitchen. "You need to be careful they don't come in through the toilet, baby," Roundhead heard Father say to Mother. She turned and stared a hole into him, as if to say, "What can I do about it?" The solution was, according to Father, to put a brick on the toilet seat to keep the beasts from swimming up the sewer line and possibly making their way into the house.

At the same time, roaches had infested the house, invited by years of neglect. They were the reason for the previous owner's cache of DDT in the cellar. By the time Little Roundhead's family occupied the house, the roaches didn't seem to be affected by the insecticide. Mother made a specialty of showing contempt for insects by flipping off her nearly weightless slippers and firing them across the room at the creepy crawlies. She had a kill rate of about 80 percent, and what she didn't kill scurried out of the room the fastest way possible.

The very thought of roaches caused Roundhead to itch. He watched them fight among themselves for a bread crumb in the dining room, and often he saw them gang up on each other as if they were teams, tearing each other apart the way some of the children did on the playground. It was horrible to look at. What were they after, anyway? Didn't they know there was plenty of food in the house for everyone, including them? All they had to do was wait. But the roaches didn't want to wait, and neither did the older boys in the community who smashed the bicycles of the younger children just for fun, or took their basketballs or their baseball bats and beat them senseless in the streets.

The roach problem escalated one morning when Roundhead, about seven years old, opened the pantry to get the apple butter out for his toast. The pantry held the family's canned and dry goods: peas, beans, stewed tomatoes, lima beans. The pantry sloped beneath the stairway leading upstairs to the three bedrooms, but because it was so poorly made, openings leading to the outside, beneath the steps, provided every kind of vermin the opportunity to come inside and feast.

On the morning he found the apple butter with its top off, Roundhead had been daydreaming about what he would do after breakfast. On his mind that morning were cloud formations. He wanted to repeat the experience he'd had the day before of tumbling down the grassy hill at the rec center, lying at the bottom face up, and watching the world spin around and around until he couldn't tell if he were on the ground or floating in the air. But the daydreaming ended abruptly when he dipped the spoon into the jar and lifted up half a dozen dead roaches, drunk on the sweetness of the apple butter.

"Mama!" he called out. "Come here, quick!" Mother, still in her slip and bathrobe, came flying downstairs and took the jar away from Roundhead. "Oh, my Lord!" she said, stirring the contents and bringing up even more of the bugs.

Something snapped in Mother that day, and within an hour Father was on his way to the hardware store to buy a new kind of roach killer that some said worked better than DDT. Simply *not* using DDT probably would have depleted the roach population in no time—they'd been thriving on it for years. But no matter what they tried, Mother and Father could never eradicate the roaches. They remained a fixture of Little Roundhead's childhood.

Over the Rainbow

Next door to Little Roundhead's house stood a sprawling apartment building where several families with children lived. Paint peeled from the building and fell into Roundhead's side yard every week. The children inside the building ranged in age from eighteen months to twelve years, but the families came and went so quickly he didn't get to know many. Among those he did know and love was a tiny girl named Lucy.

Lucy lived on the third floor. She had long, thick black hair that her mother fixed in special ways. When Lucy's mother brought her downstairs, the whole neighborhood would gather around and marvel at her beauty and energy. A chocolate-brown baby with rolls of fat bulging from her tiny legs and laugh lines already etched around her eyes,

Lucy kept the neighborhood in suspense with her latest antics. What would baby Lucy do next?

She had once put a hot lightbulb into her little mouth, where it shattered. She'd been rushed across the street to General Hospital, where they removed the slivers of glass, chastising her mother for being careless. Mrs. Lucy—Roundhead never knew Lucy's mother's name—wasn't always careful where she put things. Baby Lucy could be found toddling around the hallways with knives, cigarette lighters, oversized books. There were times when she even crawled downstairs by herself. Her mother followed, saying, "Girl, why won't you stay put?"

But baby Lucy had too much energy to stay put. She seldom spoke but she knew how to crawl and to wave like a beauty queen. Most mornings you could find her out on the third-story porch, waving to birds, squirrels, anything that moved. She was a happy baby but too restless to be called content.

Bright and early one Saturday morning, Roundhead got up at seven o'clock. The day before, he'd seen some tough little boys at the rec center pumping furiously on the cast iron swings, bragging about going "over the rainbow." One said he'd done it before—twice, as a matter of fact—and all it took was guts. Roundhead watched as they soared so high it seemed they might indeed make it over the top.

People talked endlessly about outer space in those days, and from such conversations he'd been struck by the fact that the astronauts actually practiced. Where better to test one's guts than in one's own backyard using one's own rickety swing set? Roundhead figured that if he didn't go over the rainbow, at least he would have gotten an early start on things and could try later in the afternoon. Or, if he did go over the rainbow and ended up dead, the family would have plenty of time to bury him and still see their favorite evening television shows.

The day could not have been better or brighter. Morning glories opened willingly at the touch of Roundhead's gentle fingers. These were his special flowers, and he loved them as if they were people. He skipped down to the swing set Father had installed and nervously took a seat. Perhaps he was waiting for someone to stop him, but inside he knew he had to do this—to prove that he had the guts to tackle difficult challenges. Nothing could be more important to Little Roundhead, who saw himself as the thinking person's Beaver Cleaver, than to prove to himself that he had courage.

Roundhead began to pump his little legs and to pull with his arms. As he did, he looked at the two-story home that was his and wondered just what new difficulty would present itself this day. He began to plan his afternoon, what chores he would do and in what order. First he would take out the garbage—he pumped the swing higher—then clean the downstairs bathroom, mop the kitchen floor, clean his own room. Chores were part of being a child and, as the oldest, he had more than his share of them. To complicate matters, he was expected to teach Picklehead and his newest sister, Featherhead, how to do their work as well. But Roundhead had trouble teaching. He rarely focused on one thing long enough to show others how to do it, and he often completed chores by freeing his mind to wander while he did them.

The swing set had been purchased at Sears and was strong enough to hold the boy in spite of his grandiose ambitions. But when Father put it in the ground, he cemented the legs into place haphazardly, so that the set rocked back and forth slightly, making his task even more dangerous. Little Roundhead knew that in order to make it over the rainbow, he'd have to elongate his swing so that he would end up parallel to the ground, his back hanging out and neck exposed. What were the odds he could survive a trip over the rainbow?

Within five minutes, he achieved a deep arching swing that let him sail higher than he'd ever gone in his life. From this vantage point, the clouds seemed alarmingly close, as did the treetops. He took a minute to look around, to see the world from a different point of view, when he spotted baby Lucy watching him, wearing a big smile on her face. Roundhead tried to wave, but he needed his arms to pump.

"Hi, Lucy!" he shouted. The little girl grinned. Roundhead spread his arms far apart and laughed. Baby Lucy laughed, too, and spread her arms like Roundhead's. Suddenly he felt the swing set begin to rise up on its back legs and tip forward. He glided backwards and found himself at eye level with the top bar. But going forward, the swing set tipped again, about to topple over.

The astronauts aborted missions when things went wrong, and it seemed this might be the proper time to rethink his own ambitions. He would take one more trip backwards and then bail out. So what if he couldn't go over the rainbow? He loved bailing out at the top of his flight, feeling the momentary weightlessness while he soared through the air.

Back he pumped once more, glancing at baby Lucy, who still had her arms spread wide open, but this time her tiny head appeared through the white space in the third-story railing.

"Lucy—no—stay!" Little Roundhead could barely catch his breath to say the words, and as he bailed out, kicking and clutching at the air, baby Lucy took a tumble through the third-story porch railing. She and Roundhead were in the air together, plummeting through space like falling stars, only she had no coordination and fell like a twenty-pound bag of cement. She landed with a thud, and Roundhead's frightened cries brought Mother out of the house to reprimand him for playing so early. But when she saw baby Lucy lying on the ground, she ran to the little girl's side and called out for Mrs. Lucy.

Little Roundhead breathlessly told Mother what had happened, and it seemed even to him that somehow he had caused the little girl to fall. He hadn't meant to do anything other than apply the laws of science to a backyard experiment. But another life had become involved, a precious life, and he hadn't anticipated the consequences.

Baby Lucy tumbled three stories and landed next to a giant rock that would have shattered her little skull, but she didn't even break a bone. At General Hospital, they proclaimed it a miracle. She had a few bruises and a lot more respect for the science of daredevil flying. So did Little Roundhead.

Learning the Ropes

Televisionization

Little Roundhead sat with his face so near the television that its light made his brown eyes sparkle like cupcakes in cellophane. Picklehead sat farther back. Cautious by nature, and only seven, she had heard that picture tubes occasionally exploded. Picklehead was so afraid of dying, Roundhead thought, that she didn't know how to live.

"What is that thing?" asked Picklehead, staring at the television.

"It's some kinda thingamajig the TV people put on to keep the evil spirits offa the set," Roundhead said authoritatively. "Daddy says it's called a test pattern."

"Evil spirits in the TV set!?" Picklehead scooted back at least a foot. Roundhead pressed his nose against the glass and felt the spark of tiny electrons flying off the picture tube.

"'Course! How you think they get them people inside that little box in the first place? The TV people shrinks 'em down, using their evil spirits so they can fit."

There followed a long pause during which Roundhead swore he could hear the slow, grinding sound of Picklehead's brain processing this new information. "I know that," she said finally. "But I can't see how they get from their little box to our little box."

"Don't you know nothin'?" Roundhead turned disgustedly

toward Picklehead and frowned. "The people get shrunk down and sent through the wires that come through the walls!"

"I know that," she said again, gaining confidence. "But is the same people we see, the same people everybody sees? Or . . ." Here, Picklehead trailed off trying to express an idea too difficult to comprehend. Roundhead knew what she was driving at. It had bothered him for some time now. He hadn't discovered the answer yet, but he had a theory.

"You mean," he said, leaning back slowly, "are they doing this TV stuff just for us?" He shook his head. "Nope. What they do is, the TV people send the bodies through the wires and they split into thousands of other bodies that look just like them. That way, all the people watching can see the same thing on TV. It's called televisioni . . . televisioni . . . zation."

Just then, a piercing tone that made them both scrunch their bodies up and wrinkle their foreheads came through the speakers. Roundhead and Picklehead huddled close together and started humming loud enough to block out the tone. This was the part where the Indian chief on the TV screen used his magic to keep the evil spirits that lived in the box from coming into the house. All those lines and numbers must have been some secret formula, Roundhead thought, something the TV people had stolen from the Indians. He imagined the circles on the screen related to the dances that the Indian chief did when he was angry. The whole thing must have been a purification rite, because TV had some mighty evil stuff on it, stuff he was never, ever supposed to watch. Like *The Milton Berle Show*, which they told him he was too young to understand, and *The Edge of Night*, Mother's favorite program. Later came *The Untouchables*, which the children were forbidden to even speak of, *The*

Asphalt Jungle, The Roaring Twenties, and *The Fugitive,* all presumed to be too intense for young minds.

When Roundhead was only five, Father took a course in TV repair, which he described as "real men's work," and commenced to disassemble the television in order to perfect his craft. As he learned the names of the different tubes—tubes that frequently burned out in the middle of a program and needed replacing—Roundhead also learned the inner workings of television, or so he thought.

One day, he sat next to Father in back of the set and chattered on in his usual way, asking why was there so much dust behind the TV? and where do the pictures come from? and why are the tubes so hot? and what is electricity, anyway? This last question caught Father's ear. He took a long drag on his Salem cigarette and eyed Little Roundhead. "You wanna know what electricity is, boy?" Roundhead nodded eagerly. "Touch this thing right here," Father said.

Roundhead scooted over. "Which thing?" he asked breathlessly. "This thing right here, back of the picture tube." Roundhead saw something covered with cobwebs, on which he immediately put his hand. The TV made a buzzing sound and the force from the thing knocked him backward into the wall, his whole body quivering, teeth chattering. Father chuckled. "That, son, is electricity. And you better stay away from it or it'll knock you for a loop."

If Roundhead hadn't learned about electricity in such a direct manner, he might never have discovered the evil spirits, or put together his own unified theory of televisionization. The part about the electricity splitting the people into thousands of pieces, one of which went to every television tuned to each show, came from that splintering feeling he'd gotten from the back of the picture tube.

The horrible tone stopped and the Indian chief disappeared, followed by the ghostly chimes of the National Broadcasting Company, who said they were proud to present—"What time is it, boys and girls?"

"It's Howdy Doody time!" Little Roundhead and Picklehead shouted at the TV, and for the next few minutes their faces alternated between glee and dismay. Throughout the show, the camera scanned the boys and girls in the studio audience. There were never any black faces, no one Roundhead and Picklehead could imagine as themselves, laughing and playing with Clarabell and Howdy Doody and the other characters. So the two children would quietly imagine themselves as a white child, wearing a fine dress and good shoes that didn't cramp their feet. They would transform themselves into boys and girls who couldn't be accused of looking or smelling or acting any different from the others.

But the effort required to sustain this dream often took them away from the program itself into their own private reveries. They would drift in and out of the nonsense of Buffalo Bob—the strangest-looking cowboy they'd ever seen—back into the imagined melodrama of trying to pass for white. They would see themselves arguing with their friends, shocking their parents and teachers, making big news around the neighborhood. In fact, once it was discovered that they were, indeed, white, they would probably be able to move to another neighborhood and have a three-story house with lots of flowers in the front yard.

There was an Indian character on the show, but no one took him seriously because every child in America knew that all real Indians were dead. After General Custer died in a brutal ambush, children were told, the United States Army took its revenge and wiped out the Indians. When a boy turned up at elementary school who claimed to be Indian, none of the children believed him. They all figured he was just a light-skinned Negro with "good" hair, a "Spanish" boy who wanted to be anything but colored.

By the time they'd finished their private daydreams, *Howdy Doody* had ended. Although they never spoke of this to anyone, the program that had been intended to charm them had brought forth more hurt than could be imagined. Because once the show ended, the source of their dreams vanished and they were left in the cold, hard light of reality. They were colored children, and no television program could change that.

Which is why for years, Little Roundhead got up early in the morning, dressed for school, and turned the television on long before the programs appeared. He sat staring at the lines and circles and numbers, listening to the horrible piercing tone, studying the picture, feeling good. He had decided he liked the Indian chief on the test pattern better than any of the shows.

School

One morning shortly after the family moved to Corryville, Mother dressed Little Roundhead in his gray tweed suit with matching hat and took him for a walk—no, a run—in the new neighborhood. It was too hot for the suit, which stuck to him when he sweated, and Mother was moving as if a madman were chasing them. Roundhead could barely keep up with her. She was on a mission, but she had no intention of telling Roundhead where they were going. They crossed the big street, Burnet Avenue, and went down the hill. At the bottom stood a massive brick building with Germanic gables at each corner and ugly little gargoyles around its perimeter. On the front of the building the words *Columbian School* were flanked by the numbers *1492* and *1892*.

Mother took the boy by the hand and strode into the principal's office. On the day they happened to be there, the wood floors were being waxed in preparation for the little monsters who would damage them in the fall. Mother asked to see the principal, and Mr. Herman Baldini, a short, heavy-set Italian man shook her hand and guided them into a private room. In that room was a woman—a teacher, Little Roundhead thought. He felt a surge of excitement as he looked around and saw all sorts of games and gadgets. In fact, he had never seen so many toys in one room in his life. Mother removed his jacket and the lady in the pretty dress took over.

"These are round pegs and square pegs. Can you fit them into the holes on this board?" she asked Little Roundhead, who went about the task quickly. The woman seemed impressed. She asked, "Can he read?" Mother nodded confidently and Roundhead was given a "Fun with Dick and Jane" book to read aloud. Roundhead read with great feeling and, true to his thespian nature, even created different voices for Dick, Jane, and Spot. The teacher said, "He's very mature for his age," and that was that.

Because his birthday fell at the end of December, Roundhead entered kindergarten at the age of four rather than five. The school district didn't like to admit underage children with birthdays after October 1, but in this case they made an exception of which Mother was exceedingly proud. As she told the story to Father, she embellished it a bit, saying the woman had told her Little Roundhead was one of the brightest students she'd ever met. She hugged her little boy and said magic words to him, words he would never forget.

"An education can make you anything you want to be," Mother said. "And once you have it, nobody can ever take it away from you. So nothing is more important than your schooling. You understand?"

Next came the litany of things he could and could not do in school: "Speak proper English at all times—this 'I ain't' stuff you get from your friends will not do in school. Respect your teachers. If you don't like something they want you to do, do it anyway and come home and tell us about it. If the teacher was wrong, we'll be up there letting her know she was wrong. But don't you argue with the teacher. That's not your job. Your job is to get an education."

That fall, on the first day of school, Roundhead got dressed by himself and came downstairs to have breakfast at the table. Mother checked his hands to see if they were clean and then told the boy he was in afternoon kindergarten, not morning, and he didn't have to leave for several hours. Roundhead felt such excitement at the prospect of getting an education and making new friends that he sat for hours in front of the television, just waiting. When the time came, Mother surprised him by taking him to school herself. He begged her not to, but once they arrived, he understood why she had come.

Mother and Roundhead saw what looked like thousands of black children playing on asphalt and concrete, shouting at the top of their lungs. Some played kickball, or tetherball, or foursquare, or jump rope, or aeroplane with outstretched arms, while others engaged in hide-and-seek. There were so many children doing so many things so raucously that he felt frightened and tightly gripped Mother's hand. On the way into the building, a group of older boys stood to the side and laughed at Little Roundhead, whispering things about him that he could not hear, which caused him to stiffen his back and turn his head away from them. These boys had more confidence than alley cats in a box of baby mice, but Roundhead's anxiety increased with every step.

They were the first to appear in the classroom, which gave Roundhead an advantage, because it appeared to the other kindergartners that he was a part of the institution to which they were about to pay homage. He stuck close to the teacher that first day and volunteered to do everything from erasing the blackboard to passing out little paper stars on which the children wrote their names, with help from the teacher and the teacher's new pet, Little Roundhead.

He hoped the teacher would like him, and she did, for awhile. But the more she liked him, the less his classmates cared for him, and the more trouble he got into. On the very first day, in fact, he had a shoving match with a long-haired girl with buck teeth who objected, for some reason, to Roundhead's pulling her hair. Margarete Spangling was the prettiest girl in the class, next to Diane Denora, who also had long hair but didn't inspire playfulness. Diane was smarter than everyone else, including Roundhead, and had a kind of fragility combined with haughtiness that made her a curiosity throughout their school years.

His best buddy, Francine Putnam, had nappy hair, dark skin, and a big belly. Of all the children Roundhead came to know, she was his favorite. Francine told jokes and cut up as much as the boys, but every once in a while she would stick her lower lip out and whine like a baby. This pose signified her need for attention and prompted Roundhead to make funny faces at her across the room.

But Margarete Spangling had the prettiest gap-toothed smile and a way of saying "Quit it!" that sparked his male demons and brought out a completely different side of his personality. Normally shy and reserved, he found himself clowning in Margarete's presence because she had a precisely honed sense of identity that he liked to upset. Roundhead, on the other hand, didn't know if he was supposed to be his father's or his mother's child. He had no idea whether he was brave or cowardly, smart or dumb, class clown or teacher's pet. He tried on all the parts to see which ones fit him best. In doing so, he turned himself into a classroom enigma who made kids laugh. But who was he, really?

To Margarete, Little Roundhead was a playful menace who made her first day miserable. She sat right in front of him, and from his perspective, those silky, dangling pigtails needed pulling. Margarete's hair was braided so neatly that its intricate form inspired awe in Roundhead, and the prospect of getting her attention made him wide-eyed and gooey inside. He tried ignoring her and raising his hand to answer dumb questions from the teacher: "Can anybody tell me what year this is?" Remarkably, some were slow to respond to this line of questioning, but Roundhead's hand shot up immediately, while a few others yelled, "Oooh! I know, teacher, I know!"

He also answered questions like "Does anybody know who the president of the United States is?" The teacher made the mistake of calling on Brownie Jackson, the kind of child who perpetually made a fool of himself by answering easy inquiries like this one with statements like "I know! He's the man in charge of everything!" That wasn't what the teacher wanted to know, but Roundhead soon found out that Miss X was not the brightest of teachers and often confused her students by the ambivalent phrasing of questions. Little Roundhead pointed out that the president was Dwight D. Eisenhower, a man who made little or no impression on the boy, but his nickname, IKE, kept appearing in the newspaper frequently enough that he once asked Father what IKE stood for. "Not much," remarked Father in a joke that went over his head, but later Father told him the story of General Eisenhower, a military leader who helped make the world safe for democracy.

It seems he had once been a great general, Father said, except not as great as Douglas MacArthur, who made the historic remark "I shall return." Father tried to explain what MacArthur meant, but the simple gist of it was that a white man had made a promise to some colored people that he actually kept. Eisenhower had become president, Father explained, because the man who ran against him was considered a "fairy" by some people and because it would be dangerous to have a fairy in the White House. "They all crooked," Father told him, "every last one of 'em. You can't never trust a politician, I don't care who he is. They lie, cheat, steal . . ." Which sent him on a rampage about Robert A. Taft, the Republican senator from Ohio, whose name never rolled off the tongue of Roundhead's parents unless it was preceded by several pejoratives.

Roundhead and every other child in that kindergarten classroom faced two unforgettable pictures that held an honored place high atop the blackboard: George Washington, the "father of our country," who "could never tell a lie"; and Abraham Lincoln, known as "Honest Abe who freed the slaves." These reputations for veracity were severely at odds with Father's opinion of the people who currently ran the country. And all too soon, Roundhead would find books in the library that hinted at more than a little duplicity on the part of both Washington and Lincoln.

No one in school ever mentioned the name Adam Clayton Powell—ever. By sixth grade, the names of Ralph Bunche, A. Philip Randolph, Roy Wilkins, and Medgar Evers had become somewhat familiar to Roundhead's contemporaries, but the teachers never told the students about the Civil Rights movement, which was going on right under their noses. They sang spirituals in music class like "Go Down, Moses," a favorite tune of Little Roundhead's, although its minor chords sounded distinctly Oriental. There were other songs as well, but none so consistently taught as "The Star-Spangled Banner," "America the Beautiful," and "Dixie," a hymn to the mythical South.

On the first day of kindergarten, the teacher taught the students the Pledge of Allegiance. She let Little Roundhead hold the flag, telling him never to allow it to touch the ground. This made such an impression on the boy that he thought lightning would leap from the skies and strike him dead if he accidentally dropped the piece of red, white, and blue cloth.

Roundhead had trouble with the words of the Pledge throughout his grade school career, thinking that "for which it stands" was "for Richard stands." Richard, he assumed, was yet another patriot like Paul Revere, who rode a horse, shouting, "The British are coming! The British are coming!" for which he was deified in every single year of elementary school. (Later, Roundhead put two and two together and got six when he deduced that Richard had written *Poor Richard's Almanac*, for which Ben Franklin had erroneously been credited.) Thomas Paine, Samuel Adams, Ethan Allen— Roundhead had trouble identifying with the behavior of these men because what they did never made sense to him, especially the Boston Tea Party.

As the teachers told it, fierce patriots ready to give their lives for their country dressed up like Indians and destroyed boxes of tea belonging to the British as a way of protesting English rule in the colonies. Attacking tea boxes belonging to someone else seemed to Roundhead a flagrant disregard for the law. He knew very well that if he or his friends did the same thing, it would be considered misbehavior. Yet the teachers wanted the class to admire these men, consider them heroes, and picture them as the founders of a nation committed to laws and orderly self-rule in the form of elections.

He filed this madness away in the back of his little mind and tried to focus on Betsy Ross, who, by default, became the Mother of Our Country. Here was someone to admire—yes, to love. She was so dedicated to her country that she sewed the first American flag—without a sewing machine, even— using her bare hands and a tiny silver needle. And apparently that's all Betsy Ross ever did because she vanished from American history after completing the last stitch.

Dolley Madison—who Roundhead later discovered was the most interesting, sexually repressed woman in colonial times—fared better than Betsy Ross in the fame department because there were several different snack cakes named after her. Martha Washington was not known for anything specific, but she became semifamous just for giving her husband to America without complaining of his absence.

This parade of famous people marched against the back-drop of Indian Wars, unexplained Slavery, and sudden Emancipation by Honest Abe, for which the children were encouraged to be grateful. And then there was the story of two pilgrims who played good cop, bad cop with poor little Pocahontas, an Indian girl. What was that story supposed to mean? At the age of fourteen Pocahontas fell in love with a grown white man, and he loved her back? This was too nasty for words.

None of it made any sense to Roundhead. The Pilgrims invented Thanksgiving, after which they slaughtered the very people with whom they broke bread in the Lord's name. How could the United States fight for freedom against the British while it was taking land from the Indians and enslaving colored people? The men who did these deeds were honored in ways that made them seem to Roundhead second only to God, and the students were told to grow up to be "good Americans just like Samuel Adams."

From day one, Roundhead knew something was missing from this story, but when he asked Mother to explain it, she simply repeated what he had already learned. The only hint she ever gave that she understood the real truth was a gentle, "They say George Washington never told a lie—but I don't know if I believe that."

It was another fifteen years before Roundhead realized that Samuel Adams had been a truly rabid and dangerous man, a bona fide revolutionary who bore more resemblance to H. Rap Brown than to George Washington. That's when the lights began to click on and the Great Lie perpetuated by teachers in grade schools across the nation hit home. It was all an enormous cover-up to paint the American Revolution as blessed by God himself while dozens of other freedom movements—including the bloody labor movement, women's suffrage, the Civil Rights movement, and rebellions by millions of enslaved individuals around the world—were labeled as civil unrest.

These and other unexplained contradictions might have driven him crazy if not for Margarete Spangling's pigtails. Those graceful threads of femininity were the perfect distraction from all the confusing stories his teachers told. In fact, Margarete's pigtails were just about the best part of elementary school.

Old Lady Johnson

In Little Roundhead's neighborhood, three strange women lived in a house with an unkempt yard and wrought iron gate. Only one man ever entered that house, according to legend. He was Old Man Johnson, a meek, fearful-looking farmer who'd been displaced from the country by his own lack of initiative. He didn't look strong enough to lead a team of oxen or even ride a horse. How could he plow a field? Or lead his own family? Most folks thought he couldn't.

It was Old Lady Johnson who looked like she was on good terms with oxen. She ruled the house where she lived with her grown-up daughter and her granddaughter, Faith. All three were over six feet tall, fair-skinned, and somewhat out of favor in the community. Some claimed that Old Lady Johnson had tried to kill Faith's father with a butcher knife. Others said they'd heard she'd used poison. But the real reason they weren't liked is that they were eccentric, and in the Negro community, being eccentric was like having the chicken pox—folks did their best to keep their distance.

You could tell what season it was by looking in Old Lady Johnson's back window. Spring, summer, and fall, the reclusive gray-haired woman could be seen sitting at her dressing table wearing nothing but a bra. After October, when the winds began to howl and snow swirled on the sidewalks, she'd close the windows and the shades, not to be seen again until the baby robins hatched.

No one knew why Old Lady Johnson sat in front of the window practically nude, but the back of her house faced Little Roundhead's, and he was certainly curious. He and some of the other neighborhood boys would hide behind the tree next door and stare endlessly at her bosom. She was a big woman with breasts so massive they seemed to strain the contraption she wore to hold them upright.

It was no secret that the Old Lady hated boys. The times when she caught Little Roundhead and Jeff Ruff peeking at her through the window, she would yell, "Filthy boys! Get on away from here!" and quickly pull down the shade, as if she didn't know that the whole world had been looking at her massive breasts. Evidently, exhibitionism gave her an opportunity to mix with the rest of the neighborhood, but only on her own terms.

Faith had the same attitude as the Old Lady. She rarely left the house, but if on occasion she happened to be in Gebhardt's Grocery, she seldom spoke. Neighbors claimed Faith was afflicted with some mental disorder caused by "too much inbreeding," but no one ever explained what that meant. Father told Little Roundhead to stay away from the family, that something was powerfully wrong with "Negroes who act like they ain't Negroes."

But it was more than that. The mysterious aura that surrounded these women wasn't because they spoke proper English, or because Faith was light-skinned, or even because she later wore one white stocking and one black stocking to school. No, too much bitterness seethed from the mouths of those who hated these women for their unpopularity to be about color or culture alone. Something had happened once upon a time, before Roundhead was born, probably, and the folks who kept track of such things weren't talking.

Old Lady Johnson spoke with a Southern accent. Her gray hair stood out from her head like a tattered Brillo pad, and deep, nut-brown wrinkles cut across her face like scars. As she sat before the window, combing her hair or putting on makeup, she would sing spirituals in a voice so shrill and loud half the neighborhood would chuckle, while the other half would cluck their tongues in disgust.

Little Roundhead spent hours studying this woman from a distance, and he felt in her a strange attractive power, a yearning. What people said about her—when the right folks were listening—was that Old Lady Johnson's claims to being a Pentecostal were untrue. In fact, she was a bona fide witch, like they talked about in the old days, and capable of putting a spell on you if she was angered.

At trick-or-treat time, everyone knew enough to stay away from the house with the wrought iron gate. For on that night, the house was shut up tight as a kettle drum, and no lights could be seen from the outside. Alvin Campbell, one of Roundhead's friends, swore that Old Lady Johnson had kidnapped at least one child and boiled him for dinner. Roundhead didn't believe that story, nor did he believe that the three women dined exclusively on male flesh, as some claimed.

Jeff Ruff said to Roundhead one day, "Come Halloween, I'm going to Old Lady Johnson's house and see what's what."

"No you're not," Roundhead said, alarmed.

"Bet," said Jeff Ruff, extending his baby finger and hooking it to Little Roundhead's pinkie as a symbol of his commitment. "And you going with me!"

"I'm not going up to that old lady's house, especially on Halloween," said Roundhead firmly.

"Chicken," Jeff Ruff yelled. "I thought you supposed to be a man and you scared of Old Lady Johnson's house."

"I'm scared of Old Lady Johnson, not the house. She hates boys to death," Roundhead protested. "And she won't be giving out any candy."

"Hell with the candy. I wanna look that woman in the eye and say 'Trick or treat.' And if she don't treat, I'm throwin' a rock through her window!"

Typically, Jeff Ruff had a plan with a fixed outcome and consequences for those who stood in the way of his dreams. He had a knack for deciding ahead of time what he was going to do and then doing it, no matter what. Roundhead deliberately left his goals a little vague so that, should circumstances change, he too could change without feeling guilty.

That Halloween night, all the little devils, angels, and monsters of the neighborhood honored their druidic ancestors by going door to door dressed as spooks and collecting shopping bags full of candy. There was so much confectionery in these bags by the end of the evening that parents routinely took them away from their children and slowly doled out the sweets until January. This was a warm October evening, sticky and muggy as summertime, so the parade of goblins that marched the streets and rang the doorbells was even larger than usual.

Halloween had always been a holiday that confused Little Roundhead. In church on Sundays, Reverend Holmes said the congregation should flee from badness. He regularly called down the wrath of God upon Belzabub. So why was it all right to pretend to be the Devil himself on Halloween?

Someone explained that it was all a joke, a way of scaring the demons away, but trick-or-treating carried an aura of the truly profane—Halloween was a holy day that wasn't holy at all, a day that honored demons instead of chasing them away.

In those days, it was still safe to let children go door to door alone. Those who had goodies to give left their porch lights on, while those who didn't turned them off. Roundhead and Jeff Ruff, dressed as the Devil and a skeleton, left the house about eight o'clock. There were two rounds of trick-or-treating: one for the little tykes, who left at six and were home in time for bed by eight; and the eight o'clock crowd of preteens and the few weirdos over the age of thirteen who continued to go out long past maturity, including a few adults. Some were drunkards, junkies, gangsters. Others just didn't know when to stop.

About ten o'clock, after they'd collected all their booty and eaten at least a quarter of it, Roundhead and Jeff Ruff decided to call on Miss Christian's house. Miss Christian, a friend of Roundhead's mother from nursing school, treated him like a long lost relative, and although it embarrassed him to have a grown lady kissing on him all the time, he took it in stride because the woman could cook. She baked incessantly and always had fresh cake and pie in her kitchen.

Roundhead warned Jeff Ruff not to swear around Miss Christian. "If I take you to see her and you swear, she's gonna get mad," said Roundhead, "so keep your mouth closed."

Jeff Ruff took offense. "I been knowing Miss Christian a long time, a lot longer than you. I know she don't like no cussin', I been knowing that!" he bragged. "I used to go over her house and play with that silly dog she got. So you don't gotta tell me about Miss Christian." Jeff Ruff would try the patience of a saint with his cocksure ways and loud mouth.

Roundhead warned him again. "My mother's a friend of Miss Christian and I don't want her saying that I hang around with somebody who swears."

Jeff Ruff attacked. "You just trying to get me to forget about Old Lady Johnson's house. I made a bet with you we was goin' up there this year, and you so chicken, you trying to wriggle out of it by goin' to Miss Christian's house!"

Roundhead had halfway forgotten that bet, but the details soon came flooding back to him. Now, standing between Miss Christian's house with its bright yellow porch light and Old Lady Johnson's dark and dreary mansion with the wrought iron gate, Roundhead wanted to take the easy way out. He started walking toward Miss Christian's house, not saying a word, until after he'd rung the doorbell. Jeff Ruff ran to catch up with him, but he wasn't happy about it.

"Oh, come on in! I'm so glad to see you!" said Miss Christian with a chuckle, hugging Roundhead. "How you, Jeff? Come on in, both of you. I got something special for you." They trudged to the kitchen (Jeff had a hard time walking because the corduroys beneath his skeleton costume were too big) behind Miss Christian and were seated at the table. Miss Christian proceeded to cut them each a slice of fresh pumpkin pie and pour them glasses of milk. Jeff Ruff brightened when he saw this, and Roundhead felt something he couldn't identify—a kinship with Miss Christian, as if he had a second home again and maybe a guardian angel who lived just around the block.

Miss Christian liked to take her false teeth out and put them in a glass of water while she talked nonstop about scandals in the neighborhood. The teeth sat there in plain sight, disgusting Roundhead. Yet he loved Miss Christian. He just didn't like her teeth.

After the pie came cascades of candy that Miss Christian had saved just for Little Roundhead. Jeff Ruff got some of it, but the primo stuff—Snickers bars, Reese's peanut butter cups, Bunn Bars—all went to Roundhead. "Now be sure to tell your mother I said hello," said Miss Christian as they were leaving. Roundhead assured her he would.

"All right, it's time to put up or shut up," Jeff Ruff announced. "I'm gonna go to Old Lady Johnson's house!" And he started up the hill to the forbidding corner mansion. It was now past ten and Roundhead knew his mother would be outside, patting her foot impatiently, waiting for him. "Let's hurry it up," said Roundhead. "I gotta get home."

Once they came close to the house and stood in front of it, the darkness from the yard engulfed them. Jeff Ruff hesitated at the gate, where he and Roundhead saw for the first time a tiny handwritten sign: "No Trick-or-Treaters Allowed!" "Looka there!" Jeff Ruff exclaimed. "She even put up a sign!" The two boys stood transfixed by the handwriting, which looked like chicken scratches, not at all like the writing of an adult. While they stood there, the wind kicked up a bit and the sound of the trees made them feel the eerieness of the place.

"What if she has a shotgun?" Roundhead asked.

"She ain't got no shotgun! What a woman want with a shotgun? You just scared!" said Jeff Ruff.

"Yeah, I'm scared. Aren't you scared?" Roundhead asked.

"No, I 'aren't,'" Jeff Ruff mocked his language. "I'm gonna see that woman's face on Halloween night if I don't do nothing else before I die," he said, and with that, he put his hand out to open the wrought iron gate. But it was stuck, or so he thought.

Little Roundhead hung back behind Jeff Ruff, his senses

tingling with expectation. He looked around and saw that the streets were deserted, except for a drunk slouching beneath a streetlight a block away on Melish Avenue. High on sugar, the two boys forced the gate open, breaking a latch they didn't know was there, and ambled to the front stairs. The gate closed behind them with a bang, and they turned around quickly, startled.

"What you slam the gate for?" asked Jeff Ruff.

"I didn't slam it," Roundhead whispered. "I swear I didn't."

The boys crept up the wooden stairs, pausing occasionally to listen for suspicious sounds. It seemed that only the wind was awake that evening, soughing through the trees and bushes and shrubs. Above them, the sky had clouded over, covering the stars, and the smell of impending rain wafted through the air. Jeff Ruff timidly knocked on Old Lady Johnson's door. No answer.

"Let's go," whispered Roundhead. "My mama's waiting on me!"

Jeff Ruff knocked a second time, louder and longer. Roundhead peered into the picture window, hoping to see if anyone was home. But the curtains were shut tight. "There's no one here!" he said. "We gotta go!"

"I told you, I'm gonna look that woman in the eye!" said Jeff Ruff, who knocked a third time, even louder and longer. Still no answer. Jeff Ruff turned confidently to Roundhead and said, "You see, I told you ain't nothing scary about Old Lady—"

Suddenly the door whooshed open, and there stood Old Lady Johnson in the flesh, her face horribly distorted by ghoulish makeup, white hair stretched out from her head, wearing a long ivory gown through which her Amazonian breasts could be seen heaving. "I eat little boys!" she shouted, as she rattled the front door and jumped across the threshold after them. Roundhead didn't even touch the stairs going down and tore through the thicket of the side yard, hurdling the fence and running as fast as he could, screaming all the way. "I'll cut your gizards out!" the old lady shouted, followed by gales of loud laughter and then a final call, "You better stay 'way from here, you nasty boys!"

Roundhead circled the block, his heart pumping so hard he had to stop a moment and grab his chest. As he did, he saw Jeff Ruff racing toward home, his arms pumping like Jesse Owens's. Roundhead doubled back and caught up with him a block from his house. Both boys shook like palsy victims. Jeff Ruff was bent over, holding his hand to his face. For some reason he wouldn't look Roundhead in the eye.

"What—did she bite you or something?" Roundhead gasped. "Did she suck your blood?" Jeff Ruff shook his head mournfully.

"Naw, fool," said the little Ruffian. "But she made me piss my pants!"

Roundhead looked down and saw that Jeff had indeed wet his corduroys clear through to the skeleton costume. And there was nothing left for Little Roundhead to do but fall on the sidewalk and roll in laughter as Jeff Ruff yelled, "'Tain't funny! 'Tain't funny a'tall!"

Adaptability

The roaches at 225 Goodman Street deserved serious scientific study. They ate the DDT spread by the previous tenant, took it into their systems, and made it a part of their DNA. Many died, but those who didn't adapted to its chemical structure and became stronger. They passed on their immunities to their young, who wiggled out of their roach eggs with a new hybrid vigor that made them seem virtually unstoppable—until Raid came along. Could adaptability work that way with humans, too? Roundhead thought it must, because he felt himself changing as a result of the influence of the neighborhood.

Roundhead wanted to play only if the boys would be fair and not hurt each other. Jeffrey Wesley, David Sawyer, David's brother Paul, Jeff Ruff, the too slick Mitch Powell, Alvin Campbell, Larry Pearl—the whole neighborhood of snaggle-toothed, tumultuous black boys, expressing a peculiar kind of power growing out of their physicality, played games as a means of conquering each other and evoking shame. Running over a boy during football and stepping on his head in the process seemed to make them feel better than just scoring a touchdown.

Roundhead's notion that a game needn't provoke injury to be fun meant that he was often ignored by the big, brawny, and in many ways prehistoric boys who organized such games. Roundhead had been trained to respect others, to think of people first as human beings who had feelings. Perhaps this had been the result of his early trauma in injuring Picklehead. All he knew was that buried deep in his consciousness was a desire to respectfully commune, mingle, laugh, talk, and listen to these people with whom he felt a strange, distant kinship.

Not that Roundhead was above a little mischief. On occasion, he and his friends would go to Gebhardt's Grocery and feel up Crazy Alice when she came from behind the counter. Crazy Alice liked the rough black boys who came into her father's store, though she was a girl of Appalachian stock whose eyes rolled around in her head like marbles on a skating rink. When Alvin Campbell and Mitch Powell invited Roundhead to go with them and feel Crazy Alice's butt, he agreed. While he felt her up, Michael and Tony stole sandwich bread, peanut butter, and those famous Dolly Madison snack cakes for a delicious sidewalk lunch. After doing such a shameful thing, Roundhead had trouble looking Crazy Alice in the eye.

He had agreed to do it only because he wanted desperately to be accepted, to fit in. But Little Roundhead began to understand that unless he did a thousand times more mischief—unless he changed his attitude toward the common crimes of the neighborhood—he would never be accepted. By the time he reached the age of seven, Roundhead was widely viewed as a "punk"—a scared, delicate kid who actually did his homework and loved going to school much more than pitching pennies or sniffing glue.

But in the summer of his seventh year, Little Roundhead grew tired of all the sideways talk about his thinking he was "better" than the other boys. Nothing could have been further from the truth. Roundhead felt as if he were an alien from another planet, someone who existed in the penumbra of life. He wanted to be accepted as he was, period. He didn't want to have to curse adults to their faces just to be liked by the gang, nor did he especially like "messing with girls," code for pinning them against a wall and ravaging them, touching them intimately, even raping them if no one was around to stop it. He wasn't born with a higher standard than these boys. He simply felt a deep sense of injustice and outrage on behalf of the powerless, and his parents had trained him well.

That summer brought forth a new test for Roundhead. A full-grown boxer named Popeye who lived in Monica's house, two homes up from the bottom of Goodman Street, was without a doubt the ugliest, most vicious creature ever to roam Corryville. Like all pets in the neighborhood, he was treated poorly, tied up in the front yard, fed table scraps, teased, and whipped for the fun of it. Whenever Monica untied Popeye, he ran out of the yard and chased both people and cars. In fact, he had bitten two children, but no one had done anything about it.

Little Roundhead went to the recreation center with a head full of dreams, never noticing precisely where he was going, only thinking about the fun he could have if everything went right when he got there. First, he would have to greet the boys in the right way. The right way was "Hey" or "What's happenin'" not "Hello." He would have to be careful to talk in the rhythmic language of his peers, not as he had learned to speak at home and at school. Plus, he'd need to steady himself for the jeers and curse words some flung at him simply for showing up. All of this occupied his mind, along with the possibility of playing a great game of basketball with some of the big boys, if they would only please, please, let him.

On one of these trips, he vaguely heard a dog bark. No sooner did he turn his head when Popeye leaped down the steps and dived toward Roundhead, who jumped up on the roof of a car to escape the vicious mouth of this subspecies of dog. Popeye smelled as if he'd never been given a bath, and his breath stank of rancid meat. Some said Monica fed him gunpowder to make him mean, and he'd also been known to nibble on dead rats.

Frightened, sitting atop the car, Roundhead heard Monica and her baby brother laughing at the top of their voices. "Call him off!" Roundhead insisted, which they eventually did, but they took their sweet time about it.

"I ain't never seen a boy move that fast," Monica said, laughing wickedly. "You looked like a cartoon!" Several years older than Roundhead and in junior high school, Monica sauntered down the stairs and called to Popeye. When she did, the dog returned to her—and her baby brother said, "Huh?"

Strange as it might seem, Popeye the dog had been named after Monica's baby brother's nickname, Popeye. The boy's real name was George, but he'd been born with one eye askew and wobbled about on dangerously bowed legs, a little walnut-headed cyclops who drooled spittle when he spoke. It was next to impossible to understand what he said, so Monica translated for him. Popeye the boy often barked like the dog, another point of resemblance between the two. If it was possible to be any uglier than the dog, Popeye the boy surpassed his namesake if only because he never wiped his nose with anything but his hand.

Roundhead tumbled off the car and backed slowly away, down the street, his heart in his throat. Monica tied the dog up, finally, but continued to taunt Roundhead until he made his way into the park. Once he got far enough away, Roundhead jogged into the open land of the rec center, only to hear the same vicious sound again. This time, Popeye had been let loose on his friend and next door neighbor, Clifford. With a bark more like a scream, Popeye pinned Clifford to the top of the same car, only Clifford kicked out at the dog and cursed him, which brought several people out of their houses to see what the confusion was all about. Mr. Delco, the quiet young man up the street, came down to admonish Monica and Popeye, but they didn't listen.

Roundhead stood there a moment in the park, thinking. It seemed that the dog had gotten more vicious the second time around, as if his ego had been fed by scaring Roundhead, so that his next encounter had been even more ferocious. Why should that be? Roundhead wondered. It was then he recognized the familiar pattern: like all the bullies he'd ever known, this dog grew more confident with every conquest.

Roundhead jogged around the block, circled in back of his house, and took the shortcut through Miss Monroe's beautiful garden—careful not to step on the tomatoes—into his own yard, where nothing but a few morning glories ever grew. Racing upstairs, he grabbed his treasured Louisville Slugger baseball bat with the Frankie Robinson autograph. By the time he came outside again, there was no stopping him. He walked down the street deliberately toward Popeye, the bat concealed behind him. The old dog sat curled up in a puddle of his own urine, eyes closed, no doubt dreaming of biting someone, anyone.

"Popeye!" Roundhead yelled.

"Huh?" came the human voice from within the yard, followed by the stirring of the old dog. Suddenly the dog's eyes snapped open, his haunches rose up, and he pounced down the stairs. Roundhead ran a few steps and let the dog gain on him. Monica had come out and could see what was about to happen. She screamed, but it was too late. Popeye began to run, springing forward, lunging with his head straight, like a hunting dog's.

Roundhead planted his right foot, pivoted, and met the oncoming dog with the meat of his Louisville Slugger. "Eeowwoooool!" yelped Popeye, rolling away and whimpering all the way back up the street, howling so loudly that the neighbors flew out of their houses. Monica began to throw rocks at Roundhead, but the little beanhead felt so good he even hit one of them on the fly back into the yard. When the neighbors saw what had happened, they applauded, saying it served the old dog right. Some even shook Little Roundhead's hand and slapped him on the back. "It's about time somebody took on that mean old dog," said Rodney's mother, who stood surveying the scene with her arms crossed.

After that, whenever Roundhead walked down the street to the recreation center, he never had to take the bat with him. Popeye would start to roar, and Roundhead would just stand there, daring him. Sure enough, as soon as the old dog got within sniffing distance of Roundhead, he'd emit several anemic yelps and slink away with his tail between his legs.

Roundhead had begun to shed the image of pushover by doing the kind of manful things it took to survive in his neighborhood. Deep inside, he felt bad about hitting Popeye. He wished that there had been some other way. But respect from others is tough to get, and self-respect came at an even higher premium in his community. He hadn't done the right thing by hurting that dog. But he'd done the best he knew how to do in a nightmarish world where the choices were to eat or be eaten, to beat or be beaten.

Everything Changes

What Reggie Did

Mother's little baby boy with the twinkly brown eyes was all of eight years old on that summer day when everything changed. He had become the kind of child whose classroom antics made even the most hardened teacher suppress a smile. He'd learned to throw his voice just by trying, and he could imitate the sound of a fire truck racing to a four-alarm blaze. It was good enough to stop any teacher in his or her tracks. He'd also learned to mimic the sound of the voice of the principal, Mr. Baldini, coming over the loudspeaker. He once summoned his second grade teacher to the office with this trick, and he might have gotten away with it if Margarete Spangling hadn't tattled on him.

He bounded down the steps that morning, the rec center his destination. In the valley below the neighborhood in which he lived, children of all ages were streaming toward the playground. Mostly they came to escape the tyranny of parental scrutiny. For every child in the neighborhood there seemed to be at least ten undesignated parents, and discipline could hardly be avoided when adults were around.

Except at the rec center. The unencumbered horizon line that stretched from one end of the playground to the other invited dreams and reveries. There, many a jump shot had been polished, and the electricity of forbidden activity hung in the air, an intoxicating vapor. While some children crafted necklaces out of beads and learned to swim in the outdoor pool, other children sniffed glue in the rec center bathroom, played craps against the rec center wall, pitched pennies, extorted younger kids, drank beer and sometimes whiskey if they had it.

Little Roundhead always stood back from the crowd a bit to observe the moment. He listened to the ancient spoken rhythms of his people, and the magic of the meter enchanted him every time. Now he overheard two teenage boys talking.

"I ain't got but two cents to my name!"

"Me neither."

"What he got?" They eyed Little Roundhead in the corner.

"Ask him, say, if he might could give us a quarter."

Language, the elixir he loved, was the way he understood his people. He drank them in through his pores and knew their blood was also his. But in other ways, Little Roundhead had always been an alien resident in this land. He loved books and sometimes carried them with him, even to football games in which he played. He didn't roll garbage cans or tires or pick fights, and when the others demanded that he participate in immoral activities, he cocked his head and asked, "How come?"

Something about him wasn't quite right. Father had reminded him of what that something was just yesterday. "You're just like that woman sitting over there," he pointed to Mother. "Look at you—a man don't wash his face with no washcloth. A man use his hands like this here." He demonstrated manly face washing while Little Roundhead looked on, puzzled. What made it manly, and why hadn't he known it?

How would a man react now—when the two older boys who stood towering before him bent over and grabbed his collar?

"You got a quarter?" the lighter-skinned one asked as he blew smoke in Little Roundhead's face.

"No. I don't have any money," Little Roundhead said, turning his pockets inside out. The words of his mother rang out in his head: "Always speak correctly when spoken to." But the two boys guffawed at the precision of his speech, and in the confusion that began to engulf him, Little Roundhead laughed too.

"Listen at this, Reggie! You hear this?"

"Sound like a damn white boy, don't he?"

"Sho' do." They shoved Little Roundhead to the ground and laughed again. He searched their faces for some sign of kinship and heard Mother's voice again: "Education is the way to get ahead." As he looked at their faces filled with free-floating rage, all his book learning failed him. Nothing had prepared him for this.

"Let him go," said the darker one. "He ain't worth it." But Reggie pulled Little Roundhead up and dragged him inside the rec center toward the bathroom. "I'm gonna see if you got any money hidden on you," he announced.

Roundhead didn't understand what was happening. A ruffian nearly twice his age had him by the collar, dragging him up the incline toward the bathroom. People saw it. People laughed at it. People looked away. No one did anything. Roundhead pleaded to be let go. He had to get home. Mother was expecting him soon. She'd be worried if he arrived late. But his pleas were to no avail.

Once they were inside the bathroom, the porcelain echo

of the place intensified Reggie's commands: "Drop them drawers! Bend over! Do it now!"

Little Roundhead's whimpers wafted toward the ceiling and remained trapped there as Reggie whispered, "If you don't, I'll kill you. I'll kill you!"

Reggie pulled out his thing and thrust it into Roundhead, who shuddered in pain and screamed. "Shut up," Reggie said, "or I'll burn your little ass with my cigarette!"

No longer so certain about the power of language, Little Roundhead began to stutter when he told Mother what had happened to him. Her face contorted, Mother called Father at work and told him to come home. In Father's awful presence the stutter turned into nearly terminal silence. At the police station, they had to ask Father to leave so that he could talk.

Everything Roundhead had done or said had been wrong. "You shoulda killed him, boy! You shoulda picked up something and killed him! How you let this happen?" Then Father said the words that haunted Roundhead forever after: "I bet you enjoyed it, didn't you?"

Little Roundhead didn't know what he felt. He didn't even know what had happened, exactly, but he knew that it had been wrong. That's why he told the only person he trusted. And now, in her panic, she had told Father, who called the police, who told the whole world, and the world would never let him forget.

Reggie had been a neighborhood hero—a thug who had gone to reform school and had come home after serving his time. The Friday he'd accosted Little Roundhead had been the end of his first week of freedom. He'd wanted to celebrate. Instead, after being convicted of sexually molesting Little

Roundhead, Reggie was sent back to reform school by the juvenile court. The neighborhood boys rallied to Reggie's cause. They told Little Roundhead that he should have kept his mouth shut. And they vowed to hurt him for telling what Reggie had done to him.

The court tried to protect Little Roundhead, to shelter him from the unwanted attention of these thugs. But what the court didn't realize was that Roundhead's little life—the spirit that burned inside him, kept him thinking, feeling, moving—had been nearly snuffed out by Father's reaction. Everything else the boy could take. But the utter rejection and anger Father sent hurtling his way felt like the sky falling on him and pounding him into the ground. For two days he didn't want to get up and go to school, a sure sign that he was sick at heart.

Mother and Father rarely spoke of the incident, tried to bury it as if it had not happened, as if brutality had not incapacitated their first child. But Little Roundhead suffered so much that he felt he could hear the pain echoing from deep inside. He thought of killing himself.

One day shortly after the incident, Grandmama invited Little Roundhead to come over and help clean up her backyard. When he got there, he found there wasn't much left to do except pick up some old papers and leaves. But afterwards, Grandmama fed him and sat and talked with him kindly, stroking his forehead. Finally, she said, "That was a terrible thing that Reggie done." And when she said it, she looked at Little Roundhead with the fullness of her loving brown eyes batting back tears. He knew she understood. Because it was only Saturday and she'd taken the time to make Sunday dinner a day early.

God bless her.

Revenge

What had saved and condemned Little Roundhead was the sudden intrusion of a friend, Alvin Campbell, into the rec center bathroom. Although the door was partially closed, Alvin burst in, saw Roundhead on his knees, crying, and eyed Reggie. He left quickly, yelling something, and Reggie let Roundhead get up. "You better not tell anybody," he said, a smile creeping across his face, "You better not tell — ever!" And then Reggie slithered away.

From the moment Roundhead left the bathroom, the faces of the youngsters on the playground looked distorted, grotesque. The world had instantly become an awful place to him. Each step he had to negotiate carried with it a kind of terror, each familiar landmark seemed foreign and danger-ous. He walked up Piedmont Street away from the rec center in panic, holding his pants as if he had soiled them, pinch-ing the belt around his waist so the shame would stay locked inside. He felt he might be bleeding, that a snake had gotten loose in his pants, that he might be losing his mind as the panic took over and compelled him to run. His only hope was that somehow Mother could fix it.

Mother could not fix it. The juvenile court judge could not fix it, although he tried his best. Father couldn't fix it, so deep was his own humiliation. His teachers were notified, and they did what they could to make him feel safe. When the children on the playground jeered at him, called him fag, his teachers took him aside and protected him. But their protection simply made him more of a target. Soon the whole school knew what had happened.

According to rumor, Little Roundhead asked Reggie to "bow" him, and Reggie had simply tried to give the punk what he wanted. Then Roundhead had changed his mind and squealed on Reggie. Roundhead heard this version of the story from his friend Francine, and it shocked him so much he immediately told his teacher, Miss Coyle.

"They're saying I asked him to do it to me," Roundhead wept after school one day. "Can't we make them stop saying it?"

Miss Coyle, a former nun and a strict disciplinarian, said, "You can tell them that all day, but they're still going to believe what they want."

"Why?" Roundhead cried out. "Why would they believe something that's not true?" Miss Coyle tried another tack. "Listen, young man, get a grip on yourself. People are going to say whatever they want. Your job is to prove them all liars."

Roundhead stopped whimpering. "How?" he asked.

"By being the best person you can be," she said. "Getting good grades. Making something out of yourself. Success is the best revenge. You know what I mean?"

Roundhead nodded, drying his eyes.

"Let me tell you something," she began again, this time sitting down beside him. "You have great gifts. I'm telling you, no kid I've ever met reads as much as you, speaks up in class as much—sometimes too much." She smiled. "But you also like to play around, teasing the girls, telling jokes. I think it's time to buckle down, young man, and get serious about using your talents the way you should."

What was she talking about—his "talents"? No one had ever told Roundhead that he had talent. What could *he* do?

"You know that stuff you do where you imitate other people—Sammy Davis Jr., Danny Thomas, people on TV? Well, not everybody can do that. You've got acting ability. Your papers in class show that you can write, too, although your penmanship is a disgrace. But you have ideas. Not everybody has ideas. At least not the kind you have. So why don't you apply yourself? Forget about what happened in the past. Just do your best from here on out."

Roundhead left the classroom in a trance that day filled with new hope. Because he stayed late, there were no boys lingering around to pick fights with him. In fact, the streets were nearly deserted. He thought about Miss Coyle's words at dinner that evening, where he had little to say to Mother, Father, or Picklehead. He didn't watch TV. He went to bed early, Miss Coyle's inspiring words echoing in his head, pushing out the horror.

He remembered that Miss Coyle, a mannish-looking woman with unusually short brown hair, had once been a nun and had written a book called *Pen on Fire* that traced her desire to write when she was young. Maybe she knew what she was talking about. There was no more intense person at Columbian elementary than Miss Coyle. When she set her mind to doing something, it got done. The words *flip* and *flop* were magic in her classroom. If she said "Flip!" it meant absolute silence was required. Once the boys and girls quieted down, she said "Flop!" which meant it was OK to talk again. Heaven help those children who failed to observe her verbal traffic signals. Often she paddled children right there in the classroom, in front of everyone.

Mother crept into Roundhead's room and took his temperature, pronouncing it "a little high." She wondered aloud if Roundhead had come down with a fever. "Maybe you should stay home from school tomorrow," she suggested. Roundhead snapped to attention. "No! I'm going to school tomorrow. I'm fine!" Then he fell back into bed.

The very next day, the old jitters returned on the way to

school. David Sawyer, the boy who weighed over three hundred pounds and had been held back in both the fourth and fifth grades, chased him across the big street, threatening to beat him up and take his lunch money. But Roundhead ran faster than David, and when he reached the Sheltering Oaks nursing home, Roundhead sprang into his tumbling mode, catapulting his body down the hill head over heels, the way the LSU Chinese Bandits did when they came onto the football field. David couldn't keep up.

Once he was inside, Miss Coyle called him up to her desk. "I want you to do a part in the variety show. It's a poem called "Giuseppe's Mustache," and it calls for an Italian accent. Can you do it?" Roundhead nodded exuberantly. "OK," she said. "I'll tell you more about it later."

A sudden jolt of adrenaline shot through Roundhead. Now he had something to live for, some way to prove to everyone that he deserved to exist.

The Decision

Nearly every day for the next two chaotic years, Little Roundhead dug deep and found a warrior's heart with which to fight his enemies. As the rumors about his molestation spread, boys from all over South Avondale came looking for him, and he began to understand that they spoke the same language as Reggie. They carried with them a deeply rooted self-hatred that masqueraded as cool. They looked for opportunities to call him a punk, a fag, a pussy. These words took their toll on him. When Roundhead walked to the Forest movie theater or to the hardware store, he could count on being verbally or physically harassed by someone, no matter how much he pleaded with them to understand his side of the story. The rumors stuck, and there was little he could do about it.

Fueled by his own anger, he learned to look past their supposed kinship as Negroes and to fight them with everything he had—baseball bats, knives, sticks, rocks, anything that would hurt them badly—for his salvation lay in their learning to fear him. But even this was not enough. In one incident, he knocked a boy named Garcia Montana out cold while dozens looked on. It had been a mistake. He had lost control of himself. Garcia had lunged at him, and Roundhead swung from his hip, catching the boy beneath the jaw, coldcocking him. The onlookers scattered, and the next day some of them talked about Little Roundhead as if he were a brave boy. But it didn't last. An army of ruffians thick as leaves in October came after him from all over the city, looking to defend the honor of their fallen comrade in crime, Reggie.

Little Roundhead retreated to the stillness of his inner room to read the Bible, the source of Mother's powerful wisdom. Father still spoke harshly to him, as if he blamed Roundhead for what had happened, and his rejection of his firstborn son made it difficult to talk to him with compassion. Mother loved him unconditionally, but she knew little about the male world with which he struggled. He watched as she let the pain of his molestation eat away inside her until she could do nothing but let it go. Trapped here, inside despair—a windowless room with no air, no life, no mercy—Little Roundhead calmly decided he could take no more. Dragging himself upstairs, he climbed the rickety wooden ladder to the rooftop. He had been here before, to retrieve baseballs and kites. Made of reinforced tar paper, the roof was much too fragile to support even the weight of a ten-year-old. No matter, he thought. The weight wouldn't be there long.

Poised on the edge, prepared to dead-fall into his own backyard like baby Lucy had, he opened his eyes momentarily and saw the big red ball of the sun flaring just above the horizon. He had never seen the sun like this before: a huge beam of orange light that bathed him in magnificent splendor, that washed him, cleansed him. Was it setting . . . or rising?

Confused, he sat down on the edge of the roof and stared in silence and wonder. For the first time, Little Roundhead cried and could not stop. And in the midst of the tears came a voice that said, "You have something to do." The voice startled Roundhead, and he looked around to see where it came from. All he saw was the orange sky above him, the ground below. Then, clear as any statement he'd ever heard, the voice repeated, "You have something to do!"

He paused, dried his eyes, and then backed away from the edge of the roof. He didn't know what he was walking toward, but he knew he had just walked away from death. Which meant he had chosen life in all its imperfection.

The Life of the Mind

The freeze came early that year. It was only October, not yet Halloween, and already the amber and brown of an early autumn had begun to fade, and the leaves all but disappeared. WLW, "the nation's station," predicted an early and severe winter for southern Ohio, and the winds that blew in from the north seemed unusually frigid. Roundhead's daily journeys to school grew interminable. Not only was it cold, but the heavy clothes he wore, intended to stave off sickness, weighed him down and delayed his arrival at the only port he knew would be reasonably safe in a storm.

Colored people were in the process of becoming Negroes and would soon call themselves blacks. But some people in Roundhead's neighborhood still considered Martin Luther King Jr. a radical. At school and at home Negro children were learning to speak up for themselves, to have opinions about things. They knew without being told that as they got older they would become more threatening to white society. And if they thought too much, or were too different from the crowd, they might be considered threats to black society.

Some said Negroes pushed too hard against the grain, demanded too much. Since winning the right to vote, they'd been uppity enough to seek equal education, housing, and jobs. Some even wanted to sit at the lunch counter at Woolworth's while respectable white folks ate their blue plate specials. Where would it end? The Coney Island amusement park management wouldn't allow Negroes in the swimming pool because they were said to "have a bad smell." Someone had actually been quoted to that effect in the newspapers. The NAACP wrote a vitriolic response, but it came off sounding as if Negroes had to defend themselves against even this outrageous charge. On Gilbert Avenue below massive Eden Park stood a giant billboard owned by the John Birch Society, screaming in bold letters, "Impeach Earl Warren!" That's the kind of town Cincinnati was at the dawn of the Civil Rights era.

As the snows wafted down that day in October the sickly smell of dead leaves and damp earth seeped through the partly opened window. "Your daddy wants to see you in the living room," said Mother.

In the living room, the Old Man paced like a caged lion

in a T-shirt and cotton work pants. Beneath the T-shirt, his muscles rippled gracelessly as he strode back and forth, gripping the belt as if it were a leather snake, coiled and ready to pounce. He stood slightly over six feet tall. His large, bearlike hands were callused from years of pushing brooms across gymnasium floors as a janitor. His ears were pointed like the Devil's in cartoons of the period, and the forbidding widow's peak on his forehead had recently been honed razor sharp by Miss Violet, the lady barber he visited once a week. Roundhead braced for the worst, expecting the usual fury of words and blows Father sometimes delivered on what he called G.P. — General Principles.

But when they saw each other, something happened. For a moment, the fire went out of Father's eyes as he peered at his son in pity. Roundhead stood in abject terror, hunched over, quaking, a pathetic little colored boy who was beginning to learn the essential lesson: that he was not good enough. Heaped upon the shame and fear he felt as a result of being molested by Reggie, condemned by his community, and abandoned by everyone but Mother and Grandmama, he felt Father's rebukes like iron weights on his back.

"Boy, who in the hell do you think you are, anyhow?" Father asked with genuine interest. He studied the boy quizzically, as if he had not sprung from his own loins but was instead an alien boy, brought to Earth and abandoned by Martians.

"I don't know, sir."

"You don't know?" he demanded. "Well, let me tell you who you are: you ain't nobody in this house. You may charm them teachers of yours, but you can't even take the garbage out on time! Look at it over there in the kitchen, overflowing. That's your job, ain't it?"

Father stood nearly on top of him, and Roundhead felt his hot, tobacco-stained breath in his face.

"Mister, you better get this straight: you got one job and that's to go to school, keep your mouth shut and do your chores like you're told. I don't wanna hear a peep out of you for the next month, is that understood?"

"Yes, sir," Roundhead answered quickly. Father's syntax ranged far and wide, often jumping from Ice Berg Slim to the Old Testament prophets in one sentence. When he became overly precise, as he was about to do, the message was invariably Jeremiah-like.

"Hear me, and hear me good, young man. You are on punishment from this day forth, until I say different. You are to go to school, come home, do your chores, and go to bed. If I catch you out of this house for any other reason, I'll beat your little butt till times get better!"

This was a favorite aphorism in Roundhead's house, since everyone knew that times would get better slowly if at all for Negroes. The belt uncoiled from between Father's fingers and the tension left his body. It was over. Roundhead went to his room and shut the door behind him. He was on punishment.

The life of the mind is a thing to be discovered. Like hidden gold, it waits, accumulating value until the day you begin to search for it. When Roundhead shut the door behind him that icy October day, he entered the life of the mind for the first time, never to emerge completely again. Waiting for him beneath his bed were three books he had borrowed from the school library more from curiosity than from enterprise: *Seven Plays* by George Bernard Shaw, *The Collected Works of Henrik Ibsen,* and something called *The Adventures of Huckleberry Finn, with Tom Sawyer.*

This last was such an astonishing account of a life that paralleled his own more than a century earlier that he could not put it down. When at last he finished it, huddled beneath his bedcovers with a flashlight, Roundhead felt tears of joy well up from inside. Nothing he did could choke back the knot that rose from his heart to his mouth. He buried his face in the pillow to stop the sobs, but there was no turning back the torrent. He soon cried himself to sleep.

By the second week of punishment, Roundhead had read not only *Huck Finn* but also the rest of Mark Twain's books and had begun to work his way through Dickens. Here, indeed, were other boys—white boys—who had suffered much more than Roundhead and yet somehow had endured. These were more than stories. They were blue-prints for survival in a world that seemed filled with endless cruelties.

Little Roundhead read the words aloud in an undertone day and night, mouthing them in his sleep, and soon the soothing black ink strokes across the page became a lifeline, a feeble hope to which he clung in desperation. The words transported him to a place he had never been, a place inside himself as lonely as a tomb but as comforting as the womb itself. This was his secret place, perhaps cold to others but warm to him, which he would later unveil in the arduous journey from lonely reader to lonely writer.

After two weeks of house arrest, no playing after school, Miss Coyle wondered openly if anything was wrong. "You aren't your usual chipper self," she said one day, fixing him with a too casual glance. "You sure you're all right?"

"Yeah. Fine."

"What happened to the pranks?"

"Pranks?"

"The ones you used to pull in class. You know."

"Oh. That." Roundhead shrugged. "I don't know."

Nearly overnight, he had become an introvert.

Holidays and Good-byes

Santi Claw

In the never-ending quest for acceptance waged by colored folk, knowledge became the Holy Grail. Education was said to be the key to freedom. But the more Negroes knew, the harder it was to stay sane. For instance, to speak too well in front of one's own people aroused great suspicion. They reacted as if anyone who spoke proper English was a traitor to the black cause. But to speak in the vernacular before whites was to court the shame of seeming ignorant.

The great trick of life in an integrated society, Little Roundhead began to think, was to master several different manners of speech, each one appropriate for a race or class, and to carefully consider which one to use at any given time.

In this context, Father's use of "Santi Claw" to describe St. Nicholas was little more than an assertion of his own roots. His people were from Arkansas, where nicknames were considered signs of affection.

Little Roundhead and his siblings knew little about that tradition, so the appellation Santi Claw became their only point of departure for the myth. With a flick of his vocal chords, Father managed to change the jolly old elf into a kind of nightmarish creature who sneaked down chimneys in the middle of the night to snuff out wicked little children.

Around the first of December, Father would start to sing

the song as only he could, and Roundhead would lie awake
at night trying to fathom the mixed messages:

You better watch out, you better not cry
you better not pout, I'm telling you why—
Santi Claw is comin' to town!

The menacing "better" hung in the air. Christmas was
not optional. A fat white man in a red suit was coming, and
if you didn't act just right there would be hell to pay. Father
sang it with a half smile, leering the lyrics, as if they masked
a terrible secret. But as Roundhead grew older, he thought he
had discovered the real truth about Christmas, a truth that
explained why the holiday revealed the seeds of melancholia.
That truth was revealed in Father's tone of voice and in the
words themselves:

He's making a list, he's checking it twice
he's gonna find out who's naughty and nice—
Santi Claw is coming to town!

It was Santa as hired gun, a cool but jolly fellow who took
notes on offending children and passed judgment on them
and executed the wicked. Those who were good received
toys. The ones in between, neither good nor bad, got nothing
except a reprieve from death. The bad ones were terminated.
Santa, you see, was an avenging angel. Somehow, that made
sense to Roundhead. During the Christmas season, there
were more fires than at any other time of the year. People
committed suicide, little children turned up on street corners
frozen to death, people felt lonely even in the midst of their
families. Of course! Why hadn't he made the connection before? It was because of Santi Claw, the serial killer.

Never crazy about the idea of some white man cascading
down his chimney, Little Roundhead found the tradition
ironic. Imagine the horror the reverse image would provoke

in whites. Roundhead had met precious few Caucasians whose intentions toward him were good. Most seemed indifferent, but more than a few openly sneered at him while he sat on city buses, delivered newspapers, or walked past their homes and businesses. Negroes were worse than second class—there had been no class assigned to them at all, and although they knew instinctively that whites were partially responsible for their plight, they could not help blaming themselves for what they were not or did not have.

Whites were responsible, Roundhead knew, because they had brought Negroes to America to create wealth for their own use and then took their sweet time deciding whether or not to set them free. Many whites still were not convinced that Negroes were human beings. It took time for some to acknowledge that the Constitution and the Bill of Rights applied to Negroes, too. Over the years, the stages of black humanity had progressed slowly from slavery to reconstruction to Jim Crow to "Hell, no!"

"Is Santi Claw a white man, daddy?" Roundhead had asked some years earlier, and this had brought a puzzled look to Father's face. "'Course he's white," he'd replied disdainfully. "If a colored man wore a suit like that out in public, the police would put him up under the jail!"

That Christmas Eve brought a storm of ice crystals against Roundhead's bedroom window. The crystals made noises as they fell, a hard rain of ice that left invisible patches of treachery on the highway. Black ice, cold and merciless, had caused Grandmama to take an awful skid in her new cordovan-colored Ford several days ago. "I couldn't see nothing on the ground," she'd told Mother. "Seemed like the Devil himself reached up and grabbed the car. Lord, Lord, Lord!"

At four in the morning, unable to sleep soundly for fear

that Santi Claw might be lurking about, Roundhead sat up in bed like a startled buck and sniffed the air. The bright moon-lit night hung perfectly framed by the crystaled glass that separated him from the rest of the world. Outside, the harsh wind blew, bending small trees in its path. Inside, whispered voices came floating up from downstairs. They seemed to be voices that he knew, but the boy- and girl-like giggles puzzled him. Then came the rustle of heavy paper, scurrying, and finally a pronounced "Shhh!" from a male voice.

Suddenly, the stairs leading up to the bedroom began to creak. Roundhead could tell by the cracking of the wood what stair the intruder stood on. Swallowing hard, he leaned back with one arm extended and felt beneath the bed. Behind the cigar boxes containing baseball cards and dollar bills, he fumbled for his Frankie Robinson-model Louisville Slugger, a formidable piece of lumber that he kept well positioned for just such an occasion. He closed his hand around the throat of the bat and gently lifted it into position. No light, except that of the moon at the foot of his bed, could be seen.

"Creeeeeeeeeeee," moaned the third stair softly. "Croooooook" groaned the fourth stair. "Craaaaaaaaacka," the fifth stair protested. Then came a long, pregnant pause.

"What we sneaking for? If they ain't 'sleep by now . . ." It was Father, king of the stage whisper, talking to Mother. For a moment Roundhead sat on his haunches holding the bat in the air, confused, ready to hit a home run, when suddenly Father's heavy footsteps fell naturally on the stairs, followed by Mother's shuffling gait. Because she never put her feet completely inside her shoes, Mother walked with her heels exposed, dragging leather and steel across the floor, leaving a distinctive sound in her wake. They reached the top and stood in the darkened landing like two thieves. Returning the bat to its normal position, Roundhead lay supine on top of the covers, fighting the impulse to turn over and hide his face. Not a movement or a sound did he make.

Little Roundhead could feign sleep better than a possum. Many times he had dodged a late-night whipping by pretending to be safely tucked away in the lap of the Sandman. Now, with the stakes not quite so high, he relaxed into position, fixing his face in an idyllic pose intended to communicate the innocence and wonder that transfix adoring parents in the middle of the night. The sound of Picklehead's sudden, piglike snore in the next room nearly convulsed him, but he fought off the laughter by thinking about hitting a baseball: eyes steady, hands held high but level, back shoulder upright, seeing the seams, waiting, waiting, then exploding—pow!

Father looked into Roundhead's room and studied him in the dark, unconvinced. Roundhead could hear his labored breathing, caused by the protracted climb. Father seemed to be eyeing him hard, and as he tried to relax by concentrating on another ball, a curve this time, which he took to right field—cracka!—he felt a sudden sickening feeling. This was the reason Father leered when he sang the song. Santi Claw and Father were one and the same! And now Santi Claw, the serial killer, had come to murder Little Roundhead in his sleep.

"The girls are dead out," Mother murmured from the hallway, but Santi didn't respond. He stared a hole into Roundhead, who carefully cracked one eyelid. Mother and Father both stood at his bedside, tilting their heads like Little Nipper, the RCA dog, listening to Roundhead's too-measured breathing, when Father's right hand shot up quickly and pulled the string that triggered the overhead light.

Roundhead froze. He could not have moved a muscle if he had wanted to. He saw a slider come dipping toward home plate at seventy miles an hour. Planting his back foot, he swung easily and caught it with the fat part of the bat, breaking his wrist on impact and shooting the ball through the gap in left field. He rolled over, snorted, and began to breathe regularly again.

"Ohhh, he's dreamin'," came Mother's angelic voice. Snap. Out went the light. There were few pauses now as they hurried downstairs believing that the children were sound asleep. Roundhead could hear them digging out boxes, tearing wrapping paper, fighting gently over which ribbons and bows to use for which presents. They sounded so joyful, it stunned him. So this is how Christmas really is, he thought. Mother and Father play with the presents first, then give them to the children. It must be great fun to be a parent, Roundhead thought.

Aunt Geraldine

Several weeks earlier, as the winds swirled the snow along the broken sidewalks of the neighborhood, Mother had announced that Aunt Geraldine was coming to dinner with Uncle Clay on Christmas Day. She did so with a breathless enthusiasm that wasn't typical of her. The tone of her announcement made it sound as if the queen of England were coming to visit.

Aunt Geraldine, Mother explained, was a very wealthy woman from Spain whom Uncle Clay had met while he was overseas.

"How much money she got?" asked Picklehead expectantly.

"I don't know for sure, but Clay says to make a list of the toys you want, and Aunt Geraldine will bring them with her on Christmas Day." Roundhead and Picklehead looked at each other in amazement.

"All the toys we want?" Roundhead asked.

"Two or three should be sufficient. Don't get carried away," Mother added diffidently.

"I want me one of them great big doll babies, as big as me," mused Picklehead, "and . . . and . . . and a great big doll house, too!" Mother nodded in agreement.

"I want a J. C. Huffy with colored streamers on the handlebars!" Roundhead added. This had long been a dream of his, the fantasy of mobility, of riding the wind like his other friends. He longed for the open highway and saw the streamers as wings. If only he could go fast enough, he was certain he could fly. Father, who had just entered the living room, stared at Roundhead as if he'd sworn in public.

"Boy, them bikes cost twenty-nine dollars, and that don't even include the pump for them tires. Ain't nobody gonna spend that kinda money," said Father resolutely.

"Oh." Roundhead thought again. "What if I put some of my own money to it?" This caught them by surprise. "I could give her ten, maybe fifteen dollars to make up the twenty-nine."

"You got ten dollars hiding somewhere?" the Old Man barked. For a moment, Roundhead didn't know what to say. If he said yes, he would likely lose his money to Father, who often "borrowed" to finance his thrice-weekly bingo excursions. "Well," Roundhead said casually, "I may have by the time Christmas get here." That shut Father up for the time being.

"Just remember one thing, Geraldine may come from

Spanish money, but her address is not Fort Knox—least not last time I looked," Mother said.

Roundhead couldn't help being dizzy with excitement at the prospect of receiving two extra gifts on Christmas Day. And this from a woman he didn't even know.

"Who is this lady again?" Picklehead asked. Mother smiled. "She's the woman that's gonna make your Uncle Clay a happy man again."

Clay had been a pilot in the navy during the Korean War. Somewhere over North or South Korea, so the story went, his plane had caught fire and he'd ejected, landing in a rice paddy behind enemy lines. For six days he hid in the tepid water, eluding the enemy, hoping to work his way back to safety. Instead, he was captured by the North Koreans and tortured in unspecified ways.

Since then he'd been ill, by all accounts, and although no one knew precisely what was wrong, Roundhead knew that Uncle Clay was "not quite right in the head." The halting manner in which he spoke, the way he avoided looking people in the eye, the affected demeanor of someone trying to look casual when everything is falling apart, gave it away. He had a permanent account at the VA hospital where he went for painkillers and psychiatric treatment. Nothing worked as well as drink to ease the pain, but when he developed a bleeding ulcer, even alcohol betrayed him. The children were under strict instructions never to utter the word *rice* in front of him.

"Mama, how we even gonna talk to this lady? Don't none of us speak no Spanish," said Picklehead. That Picklehead—she thought of everything.

"Never you mind. Clay speaks Spanish, and he'll do the talking for us."

This comment raised serious doubts in Roundhead's mind. Clay could barely speak English. But the family lore did include the story that while Clay was in a military hospital in Spain recovering from his ordeal, he had learned the native tongue well enough that he'd decided to remain overseas awhile. He had placed cryptic calls to Mother saying he "couldn't make it back," that it was "no good trying to live in the States anymore," that he would only get in trouble if he returned.

But Clay soon drifted back home. Miserable, with no job, and in nearly constant pain from his tortures, he tried to drink himself to death. The government took pity on Clay and gave him a job as a postal worker, lifting heavy bags eight hours a night. It was enough to keep him awash in alcohol, but Uncle Clay was slipping badly. There were days when he could not leave his house, when Grandmama would call and say with a deep sigh, "I got to go over there again and see about that boy. He gonna be the death of me yet."

Aunt Geraldine had apparently changed all of that, which was a miracle, to hear Mother tell it, too good to be true according to Father. And now this lady from a culture so foreign to the family that it could scarcely conceive what she looked like would soon grace their home, bringing gifts straight from the throne of Queen Isabella.

Bright and early that Christmas morning, the telephone rang. Grandmama informed Mother that she was about to leave the house in her new car, which she babied as if it were human.

"I'm picking up Clay and Geraldine, then I'll be on over. Shouldn't take more than an hour or two." Grandmama only lived ten miles away, but the way she drove, the family would be lucky if she arrived in time for dinner.

Meanwhile, the children took baths and got dressed before coming down to open gifts. Featherhead, the newest addition to the family and only five years old, kept chanting, "God is good, God is good," as Mother scrubbed her neck. This was her mealtime Bible verse, which she repeated anytime she grew impatient and wanted to dispense with the business at hand.

Once they were "presentable," as Mother liked to say, the children were expected to walk down the stairs like good middle-class adults, not run like "heathens," and sit quietly in the living room. The children knew Mother and Father could not afford much and they were grateful for whatever they received. This year was a particularly light one for Roundhead: a wooden mop-handle hobby horse and a Winchester air rifle. There was definitely a western motif about the gifts, which puzzled Roundhead since he had taken great pains to make it clear that he was now into sports, not cowboys.

They cleared away a big spot under the tree for Aunt Geraldine's gifts. Picklehead had purchased a perfume called Longines with Mother's help, and Roundhead had found a book on Spain that he thought she'd appreciate. Father argued that since the book was in English, it was inappropriate. "'Sides, what she want to read about her own country for? You shoulda got a book about America." Maybe so, but it was too late now.

Within the hour, they heard the car door slam and instantly the children shot to the window. Before they could catch a glimpse of Aunt Geraldine, Mother had them by the scruff of the neck. "No you don't! Sit right back down on that couch and act like you got some sense!"

Grandmama, Gran'daddy, Mr. Gene, and Uncle Clay came through the door smiling broadly. "Merry Christmas!"

everyone shouted. "Give me some sugar, baby!" Grandmama demanded as she smooched Roundhead, slobbering on his cheek. Mr. Gene pumped Father's hand and grinned a toothless grin. "Hi you doin', professor?" Father greeted Gene. Mr. Gene, the only real philosopher Roundhead ever knew, had theories about everything. His current belief, about which the family heard a great deal that Christmas Day, was that the launching of the Telstar satellite had caused the early winter.

"How you get here so fast?" Mother asked. Gran'daddy chuckled. "Geraldine drove. Your mother liked to had a fit 'cause the speedometer touched forty-five," he kidded.

"That girl can drive, can't she? She can sho' 'nough drive. She can motor. That girl can drive—uh-huh, uh-huh." It was Uncle Clay speaking, his eyes rolling back in his head weirdly as he made his point.

"Well . . . where is she?" asked Mother expectantly. They turned to the door just in time to see it flung open. A coffee-colored woman in a tight wool sweater, dark pedal pushers, and open-toed shoes leaned in carrying two packages. Her short black hair had been greased back like a man's, and a cigarette dangled precariously from her ruby red lips.

"Clay, get the door! Lord have mercy, you leave me outside like a common criminal, about to freeze my butt off!" She looked up. "Oh—'cuse me," she muttered. "I know I shouldn't cuss in front of the children. Hi y'all doin'?" she beamed and stumbled in, dropping ashes all over the floor. No one uttered a word, except Picklehead, who looked up at Mother in astonishment.

"Mama, this lady speak *good* English!"

Pinching Picklehead with one hand and extending the other, Mother was right on time with the social graces. "How do you do? We've heard so much about you. It's so nice to have you here in our home."

"I am glad to be here, honey—it is so cold over at Clay's place," she said. Awkward introductions were made all around, and when she got to Roundhead, the only boy child in the family, she gave him a special greeting. Grabbing his head, she forced it between her breasts and hugged him close to her warm, round body. "Child . . . I have heard so much about you it ain't funny! You and me gonna be good friends!"

"Well," said Mother, her hands aflutter, "I certainly hope so."

"You the smart one in the family," Geraldine said, grabbing Roundhead in a playful hammerlock. "Your Uncle Clay be braggin' on you 'least once a day, chile. Y'all got an ashtray?"

It was difficult to place her accent but everyone knew they didn't speak English like that in any part of Spain. As the adults strolled into the dining room, Picklehead tugged Roundhead's sleeve. "Where the presents at?"

"There's too many of 'em to bring in at once! She left 'em in the car," Roundhead speculated. "Don't you dare ask for 'em or you'll spoil the whole thing." She put her finger to her lips and nodded.

Mr. Gene gave his customary Christmas gift to each child—a shiny new silver dollar. It was his habit to polish them personally for Roundhead and Picklehead, then drop them in their laps while saying, "Bet that one don't bounce!" Everyone would laugh as if they understood the inside joke.

Christmas dinner was served no later than two o'clock in the afternoon. The table lay spread with turkey, ham, candied yams, mashed potatoes, creamed corn, collard greens with fatback, cranberries, pickle relish, and corn bread dressing made with the liver, gizzard, and heart of the bird. Grandmama cooked most of the food because Mother, bless her heart, could not cook to save her life. At least two kinds of pies, often three—pumpkin, sweet potato, and mince-meat—graced the table.

The three children, Roundhead, Picklehead, and Featherhead, sat in the kitchen during dinner, straining to hear the adult conversation.

"Now, Geraldine would burn gravy. Yes, she would! I'm tellin' you she would burn gravy! Whoa—I ain't lyin'," Uncle Clay said.

"I ain't got time to cook. You wanted you a cook, you shoulda found you a Swedish gal," Geraldine retorted.

"Where are you from, Geraldine?" Mother inquired cheerfully.

"Well," she said, smacking the turkey grease off her fingers, "a lot of different places. I was born in Alabama but we followed my daddy all over the country when we was little," she said.

"What line of work was he in?" Father quizzed.

Clay guffawed. "Tell him what line of work. Tell him!" he chortled. "You ain't gone believe this! Go on, tell him!"

Geraldine took a long drink from her third bottle of Hudepohl beer. "Clay, if you don't quit!"

"Go on—tell him what line of work! Go on!"

"My daddy was in prison."

At this, Roundhead poked Picklehead hard in the ribs. "What?" she shouted, her mouth overflowing with applesauce.

"Listen!" Roundhead whispered.

"My mama and the rest of us used to follow him around when they moved him from place to place, me and my three brothers. He was a bad man, they tell me, but he never done me no harm."

Grandmama tried to change the subject. "How you like them cranberries, Mr. Gene?"

"All right," said Gene flatly, not looking up from his plate.

"What was he in for?" Father asked.

"Go on—tell him what he was in for! Go on—tell him!"

"Clay, shut up and let the lady talk," said Gran'daddy.

"They say he killed a man at a truck stop one time," sighed Geraldine. "But I never did believe it. I think they framed him, like in them murder mysteries. He claimed he wasn't nowhere near where they found that man. I believe he was telling the truth."

"Probably so," said Father after a long pause. "They all the time framing Negroes, especially up north nowdays."

"Ain't that the truth?" Geraldine exhaled smoke. "Fact is, if there was something to do down in Alabama that payed a decent wage, I'd go on back down there in a hurry. At least there you know where you stand with them folks when you cross the Masie-Dixie line. But I'll be damned if I'm working in some catfish factory for seventy cents an hour!"

"You ain't got to worry, baby, 'cause I ain't goin' to no Alabama come hell or high water. No sir, I ain't goin' to no Alabama. Uh-uh, not me, no sir! So you ain't got to worry 'bout that!"

"Mo' greens, Juanita!" Mr. Gene demanded, passing his plate. The family often remarked that if Mr. Gene could have found a way to eat the design off his plate, he would have.

After dinner, the cha-cha records came out. A popular dance among adults at the time, the cha-cha seemed made for Aunt Geraldine. She swung her wide hips freely to its

Latin beat and made no pretense of hiding the feelings it inspired in her. Swiveling to the music, she moved from partner to partner in the small living room, even grabbing Father at one point and dancing around him in a show of raw sexuality. He stiffened when she touched his shoulders and began to move in place like a man nailed to the floor.

Mother shot him a glance that would have withered an evergreen, but that wasn't the reason he froze. He froze because Geraldine took the lead and forced him to follow. Feigning exhaustion, he finally dropped out, and Geraldine moved on to Roundhead, twirling him about like a beanpole as Picklehead, Grandmama, and Gran'daddy looked on in amusement. When the music ended, she dipped Roundhead back like in the movies, and everyone applauded.

"Where you learn to dance like that?" she teased. "Not watching your mama and daddy," she said, throwing her head back and laughing. "Your Uncle Clay can dance, too. Can't you, Clay?"

"Me?" Clay asked, thoroughly soused by now. "Not me. Uh-uh—I can't dance. No, sir. Not me. Uh-uh."

"You could if it was just me and you—couldn't you?" she asked seductively. Nat King Cole's "Straighten Up and Fly Right" played in the background as Geraldine grabbed Clay and dragged him to the middle of the floor. He protested weakly but Geraldine stood him up anyway and pressed her body close to his. He began to giggle and to lean into her in a slow dance played against the rhythm of the music. They held each other tight and circled round and round in some kind of ritual, Geraldine on tiptoe, her thighs grinding hard against his. Roundhead felt the blood rush to his cheeks.

"Well," Mother said brightly, "why don't you children go

get Geraldine her gifts. Won't be long and she'll be going home."

This was the wrong time to leave the room, but Roundhead did as he was told. When he returned, Geraldine sat on one side of the room and Clay on the other, wearing long faces. Mother and Father both had their hands folded, like school principals do when they've made up their minds to punish someone. Mr. Gene was slumped over in the rocking chair, sound asleep. Gran'daddy mumbled, "They didn't mean no harm," which brought a sharp retort from Grandmama: "Not in front of the babies!"

Roundhead had decided to make a little speech before presenting Geraldine with her gift. Who knows where such instincts originate? There was nothing in his family to suggest that speech making was expected or even appreciated, but he had something to say and began with a joke.

"Aunt Geraldine, I wanted to buy you something real nice for Christmas, since this is the first time we met. But the tooth fairy forgot to show up this year." He paused, looking at Father in mock sternness. Even the Old Man chuckled. "So, instead, I just got you this book." Roundhead handed her the book, by now a bit dog-eared from the nights he had read it under the covers.

"*The Life and Times of Queen Isabella*," Geraldine read in a monotone.

"You see," Roundhead said evenly, smiling, "we thought you were some rich lady from Spain."

"What you mean, Spain?" she asked indignantly. Roundhead looked at Mother helplessly.

"What the boy's trying to say is, we were told—that is, Clay led us to believe that—you, uh, were from another country. He told us about you being related to the Spanish queen and all." Mother hesitated. Geraldine, slightly inebriated, sat upright in the chair.

"I guess that wasn't right," said Mother. "Now that we've met you, we can see that you're an ordinary colored woman just like the rest of us."

Lord, why did she have to go and say *that?*

"Well, I'm real sorry," Geraldine answered curtly. "But I think you got me confused with that crazy white girl Clay used to know. The one he met when he was in the psych ward," she spat. "She ain't from Spain, either. She's from Erlanger, Kentucky! But she can say she from anywhere and fools like you will believe her!" Geraldine bolted out of her chair. "Come on Clay, we got to go!" She woke him with a kick to the shins.

"But what about the presents?" Roundhead shouted involuntarily. Geraldine pulled Clay up by his lapels and grabbed his arm as he stumbled behind her. "Keep 'em!" she said, tossing the book to Roundhead and dropping the perfume in front of Picklehead.

As they gathered their coats and moved toward the door, Geraldine looked especially weary as she said, "I don't know whether you know this or not. But when Clay was in the hospital, he couldn't even clean his own behind." She smiled. "That's how we met. Romantic, ain't it?" She left indignantly and never returned to their home again.

Roundhead knew why there had been no gifts. Geraldine was not from Spain. She was from Alabama. She had never heard of Queen Isabella. And she was far from rich. She wasn't even Roundhead's aunt because she and Clay never married. She was just a coffee-colored black woman with liver spots on her face and bright red nail polish on her fingers and toes. Roundhead was sorry to see her go.

Fallen Angel

On July 4, 1960, five months short of Roundhead's tenth birthday, the family went back to 418 Elizabeth Street for an old-fashioned celebration of Independence Day. This meant the house would be overflowing with uncles, cousins, nieces, and nephews, a veritable stampede of people loosely connected with Gran'daddy through work and drink, and a few quiet visitors from Grandmama's side of the family, like Aunt Betsy. Grandmama liked to cook and watch everyone else eat. On the menu this day was steamed fried chicken, barbecued ribs, hamburgers, potato salad, cole slaw, sliced tomatoes, onions, carrots, and Wonder bread, which, they knew from incessant repetition of the TV commercial, "helps build strong bodies twelve ways."

Aside from this claim to improve the health of growing boys and girls, Wonder bread had another advantage at a barbecue. Soaked with the special hot sauce grandmama cooked up, two pieces of Wonder bread became a delicious side dish. In actual fact, the stuff was so devoid of nutrition it wouldn't even grow mold. He knew this because he'd found pieces of it in the garbage can days after it had been placed there, and even the maggots rejected it.

The highlight of the day, the Knights of Columbus parade, took place downtown, on Court Street. The Reds were playing a holiday doubleheader on television, but Mr. Gene, baseball purist that he was, turned the sound down on the television so he could listen to Waite Hoyt, voice of the Reds. Hoyt had been a friend and teammate of Babe Ruth and a great pitcher for the Yankees back in the 1920s. His beautifully told stories about the good old days of baseball, the cutups and characters he knew, made Cincinnatians pray for rain delays. Roundhead learned as he listened about the fascinating connection between baseball and the American personality, both of which still had a bit of innocence left in them.

But before the game began, Mr. Gene and Gran'daddy took Roundhead and Picklehead to see the parade. Father and Mother soon followed. People brought chairs to sit in just to watch the armies of marchers with their uniforms and medals. The noise from blaring trumpets and drums was far too loud for Picklehead, who had to be taken home. Roundhead didn't get spooked until the Knights of Columbus themselves marched by and he saw the strangest collection of white men in uniforms with sabers and rifles he'd ever laid eyes on.

Roundhead asked Mr. Gene who they were, and he snapped, "Just a bunch of Catholics showing off." But something about them appeared foreboding. Perhaps it was the different flags they carried—one American, one Confederate, and another with the K of C logo on it. Perhaps their severity startled him. Most of the groups waved to onlookers as they marched by, but the Knights of Columbus took themselves so seriously that each and every member looked as if the parade were a sacred rite. To top it off, the final color guard came through shooting its guns in the air, which frightened Little Roundhead so much that he plugged his ears and watched as the last of the white men in uniforms and plumed British naval hats marched by.

Roundhead went back to Grandmama's house with the parade ringing in his ears. He was ready to eat the steamed chicken, barbecue, and sweet potato pie she'd prepared. But instead of serving the food, the grown-ups sat around out on the patio, fanning themselves, talking nonsense. So hungry he could feel the sting of gastric juices, Roundhead was forced to endure adult conversation at a time when he should have been eating.

"That sure was some parade, wasn't it?

"Yes, indeed."

"You shoulda seen the parades years ago—much better than these ones they been having last three, four years."

"Mr. Gene, what's the difference? A parade's a parade, ain't it?"

"Oh, no! We seen parades with royalty in 'em. With all kinda different horses—Arabian stallions, Lipperzanners—the kind that prance up and down when they walk," said Gene.

"Bet there ain't never been no colored parade," someone said.

"Sho' there's been colored parades! Sometimes, on the Fourth of July, they'd let our boys march with the rest of them."

"They ain't done that since 1918, when the boys come back from the war all prettied up in they uniforms."

"Them was some times." Gene let the memory sink in. "Yes, sir. For a while there, look like we done turned the corner."

Mr. Gene meant that after colored boys had spilled their blood and given their lives under General John "Black Jack" Pershing in Europe, they came back to the States feeling fully equal and expecting their rights as Americans. What happened instead was a determined effort to keep the Negro in his place, buttressed by violence all over the nation. The Ku Klux Klan, once dead, started up again in the neighboring state of Indiana in 1920, even more menacing than before the war. In Cincinnati, there were riots in which decent, law-abiding colored citizens falsely accused of planning an insurrection lost their property, and even their lives.

Returning Negro soldiers were attacked at the train station in Chicago by angry whites who felt threatened by the prospect of free sable-colored Americans trained to use deadly force. But the 1917 Brownsville, Texas, hanging of black soldiers accused of mutiny deadened the hopes colored Americans had for equality. President Wilson refused to intercede or condemn the hangings. And although some colored soldiers were briefly allowed to march with white soldiers, the practice didn't last long. Evidently, World War I had not been the war to end all wars, even at home.

This history was the farthest thing from Little Roundhead's mind on July 4, 1960, Independence Day. He felt drowsy that evening from the overwhelming heat and the stress of the parade. He ate, played marbles with some of the neighbor boys, and fell into a deep sleep as soon as his pea-shaped head hit the pillow.

He awoke early in the morning to hear his Grandmama crying. Not loudly but softly, as if each tear hurt as it emerged. Daylight had just broken, and the sun had barely peeked over the horizon. Ordinarily, he would have awakened earlier to the sounds of the Silvertone Gospel singers, a radio quartet that entertained Grandmama and Gran'daddy around five-thirty. But no radio played this morning.

Little Roundhead heard Mother trying to comfort Grandmama in the hallway. He heard her say it would be all right, everything would be fine, and that prompted him to get out of bed to see what had happened.

"Go on back in your room now," said Mother with a trace of irritation.

"What's wrong?" Roundhead inquired.

"There's been an accident," said Mother. "Go on now. I'll be with you in a minute."

Roundhead sat up ramrod straight in his nightclothes, considering every possible scenario, alternating between the hope that Father had abandoned his family to the fear that something had happened to his baby sister, Featherhead. But soon Mother came and told him the news.

"Your gran'daddy had an accident. He's in the hospital. We don't expect him to live." Mother disappeared like a ghost. To say she evaporated would be no exaggeration. Her image and the expression on her face lingered in Roundhead's mind long after she left the room.

The boy fell back on the bed and sobbed. Gran'daddy Willie, who had been so happy just the night before, had gone without saying good-bye. He could still see his grinning face, the face that had kissed him many a time, the arms that had picked him up and sat him on his knee. This was the man who first took him fishing, who taught him how to bait a hook and teased him mercilessly by pretending that catfish knew how to meow.

Three days later, Gran'daddy died a painful death in Christ Hospital. Mother told Roundhead that he had broken his neck in three places. Grandmama made cryptic remarks like "God let him suffer for his sins." Roundhead listened intently, trying to pick up what had actually happened to Gran'daddy, but the family wouldn't say a word, nor would they let him go to the funeral. A few days after Gran'daddy had been buried and they'd gone back to Goodman Street, Roundhead made further inquiries of Mother.

Mother never lied to Roundhead. She felt that his spirit was so much akin to her own that she could do nothing but tell him the truth. But this particular truth hurt Mother, so she measured it out piecemeal. First, she told Roundhead that Gran'daddy had been sleeping outside on the steps of the brownstone when he'd turned over and fallen off the ledge into the basement and broken his neck. Later, after Roundhead had digested this, he asked, "Why was Gran'daddy sleeping on the steps?" The answer—because Grandmama had locked the door—only confused matters.

No one wanted to say that Gran'daddy Willie had been drunk when he came home that night. His wife had told him that if he ever arrived too late, she would lock the door. Midnight had been her curfew. Gran'daddy Willie missed it then as he had several times before. Grandmama knew that when he was drunk, Gran'daddy Willie was apt to start trouble. He came home flailing and bitter and armed with a sailor's vocabulary. She never could tell what he would say or do, and she always felt in danger when he fell into the house stinking of tobacco and whiskey.

On this particular evening, she had her grandchildren to think of. And she knew in her heart of hearts, with the kind of certainty reserved for saints and prophets, that there was nothing she could do to stop Gran'daddy Willie's march to death through the bottle. She knew in her fingertips from caressing his wavy hair that Gran'daddy Willie was a simple country boy who had lost his way in the big city. He had come to Cincinnati to make money because the white men in Georgia wanted to take his job away. He left to keep his pride but sacrificed himself to the machine culture of the modern city, the urban factory, where he made pieces of steel that fit into other machines. The factory's tedium started Gran'daddy's descent into the escapist subculture of the colored underground, where men who work at monotonous tasks go to create meaning, even if it's artificial. But what killed him was Grandmama's decision to lock that door. And because he didn't have a key or a place to sleep, he curled up on the ledge of the brownstone he owned and took one turn too many in his sleep.

What must he have felt as he fell, over and over in the heavy night air, his rumpled coat extended like angel's wings? Surely, thought Roundhead, Gran'daddy Willie could have flown—if only he'd known how.

New Year's

Gran'daddy Willie had gone, and Grandmama purposely turned to Roundhead to be the man of her house. Every household needed a man, she said: you never could tell when there'd be something heavy to move. And every now and then, you might just want to have an argument with someone you cared about.

Mr. Gene continued to live with Grandmama, but he was much too smart to argue with her. Over the years, he fell into a Buddha-like silence that reflected both his wisdom and his hearing problem. Grandmama didn't believe Gene was hard of hearing. "If you whisper 'dinnertime' anywhere near this house, Gene will be at the table," she said.

Gene still took care of Grandmama's bills by walking downtown every couple of weeks and paying cash for the gas, the electric, the telephone, and such. Colored folks were funny that way in Cincinnati. The older they were, the more likely they were to distrust banks, and many kept their money in secret places.

In fact, before Grandmama could move from the house at 418 Elizabeth Street into her new duplex on Highland

Avenue, she faced an enormous challenge. For years, she'd taken Gran'daddy Willie's money out of his pockets when he was drunk and stuffed it into the cracks in the walls of her kitchen. Many times she would forget precisely where she put it. But if anyone could find money, it was Grandmama, who had all the business smarts of a big-time banker but a better sense of humor.

A good Methodist most of her life, Grandmama believed in the basic Protestant principles of moderation and practiced them routinely: she didn't smoke, seldom drank, and dressed well in public so that "the faith would not be spoken of abusively." She expected to go to heaven when she died and believed that rules and regulations were in place to ensure that only the right people would be there with her.

But Roundhead knew that this was no ordinary Grandmama he was dealing with, either, because there were times when she spoke of things that did not seem to be solidly within the Christian tradition. She believed in hants, ghosts, witches, and warlocks. She claimed many times to have seen ghostly figures at the foot of her bed doing odd things, like walking backwards and counting to a thousand by tens or calling her name out loud. Grandmama volunteered these bits of information in the middle of dinner, as when she once said, "Had a visit from Mr. So-and-So last night. Came right through that wall over there."

Mother and Father always ignored these comments, as if she were a child caught up with weird fantasies. Transfixed by the details, Roundhead waited to hear more. But Grandmama didn't especially like to tell her secrets in front of people who didn't believe them, so she kept them to herself. Until Roundhead came over to do the chores.

Once every two weeks or so, Roundhead hopped on the bus and went to Grandmama's house to rake, paint, pick up stones, bundle sticks, whatever needed doing. But mostly he went to Grandmama's house because she liked to talk and encouraged him to do the same. She paid him five or ten dollars, but the money wasn't the attraction—Grandmama was.

"I declare, boy—you done growed up!" she'd say, rubbing his head. "What you been doin'? Eating double like you used to?"

"No, ma'am. Not since we left Elizabeth Street."

"Well, you looking mighty good. Come on in here, let me take a good look at you." Roundhead always felt slightly embarrassed as Grandmama made him turn around so she could examine him.

"Mighty fine lookin' young man. Want you to help me wash these windows today. They look a fright."

These routine visits kept Roundhead connected to the softer side of his family, Mother's side, where there seemed to be an infinite supply of mercy and tenderness. But there were other visits that were anything but routine. They began the New Year's Day after Gran'daddy Willie died.

"Mama wants you to come over to her house this morning," Mother said to Roundhead about eight in the morning on New Year's Day. "Come on and get dressed."

Roundhead paused. "How come?"

Mother said, "Because she needs you now. All you got to do is what she tells you. She said she'd give you seven dollars."

Roundhead dressed, thinking to himself that this didn't sound right. Seven dollars to go to Grandmama's house? For what?

Mother called a taxi, which sped over the hill and down

Highland Avenue so fast he didn't have time to get anxious. As the cab pulled away, Grandmama opened the door.

"Hi, big boy! Come on in."

"Hi, Grandmama. You sent for me?"

"I sho' did. I got some nice cookies up here in the jar—"

"But Grandmama, it's so early in the morning. Nobody's even out on the streets."

"Never you mind. Now, come on in."

Roundhead walked up the stairs pulled by the savory smell of a fresh pot roast in the oven. He peered in the corner and saw Mr. Gene, already dressed, sitting in his room, looking out at the street below. Gene had his plaid shirt buttoned at the collar, his long underwear peeking out from underneath. "Howdy, Mr. Gene." Roundhead went to shake his hand, and Gene patted him on the back of the neck. "How you doin', boy?" Then Gene went back to staring out of the window.

"Now, I know you don't understand what this is about, but I'll do my best explaining it to you, sugar," said Grandmama. "See, it's very bad luck if you don't have a man walk through your house first thing New Year's Day. Very bad luck. So, since Willie ain't alive it seemed best if I found a man to do the job."

"Me?" Roundhead protested. "I'm not a man."

Grandmama laughed. "You may not be growed up all the way," she smiled, "but chile, you a man. I know 'cause I seen a few of 'em. So, what I want you to do is walk through the house now—slowly—don't be runnin'. Oh, and take that coat off and throw it over yonder."

Roundhead slowly took one step after another, first through the dining room, where Grandmama led him around the table. Then he paced the living room floor,

around the perimeter, into Gene's room, back again into
the kitchen and finally the bedroom.

"Ah, that's good!" said Grandmama. "Now I'm bound to
have good luck all year, thanks to you!" She kissed his cheek
and then said his favorite words.

"Let's see what I got in the oven!"

Jesus Wept

Baptism

Little Roundhead first met the spirit world at the bottom of a chlorine-drenched swimming pool in 1962. He'd known that God existed chiefly because two autumns before, the Pittsburgh Pirates had beaten the hated New York Yankees in the World Series. And in 1961, the hometown Cincinnati Reds won the National League pennant. This was all the proof Little Roundhead needed that a supernatural being directed the universe.

But faith can often be a fragile thing. And so it was that the following spring, the season of renewal, Little Roundhead sat on his front porch struggling to read a new book when his best friend, Jeff Ruff, laid bike rubber in front of his house and yelled, "Whatcha reading now, homo?"

Little Roundhead slowly lowered the book and stared hard at his friend. Even Jeff Ruff hadn't forgotten about it. Little Roundhead was still forced to defend himself against fierce accusations.

"You liked it!" some said.

"You asked for it!" others yelled.

What they could not know was that Little Roundhead had made those same hateful accusations of himself.

Jeff Ruff spat through the gap in his front teeth and grinned, knowing he had struck a nerve. To call a boy a homo in that day and age was an invitation to duke it out. But Little Roundhead remembered Mother's admonition — "Always consider the source" — and took comfort in the fact that Jeff Ruff was like Eddie Haskell, the kind of boy every parent despised.

The brand new J. C. Huffy bike Jeff sported caught Roundhead's attention. "Where'd you get that?" Roundhead asked.

"Sears," came the sarcastic answer. "Where you think?"

Little Roundhead descended the stairs to get a closer look as Jeff Ruff absentmindedly dug boogers out of his nose.

"It's bad, ain't it?" Jeff Ruff grinned proudly.

"I bet you stole it, didn't you?"

"That's for me to know and you to find out!" Jeff Ruff said, but Little Roundhead wouldn't let go.

"You expect me to believe your daddy bought this?"

"Naw," Jeff Ruff spat again. "I bought it my damn self!"

Gradually, the story unfolded. For several months now, Jeff Ruff had been abusing his position as a member of the Second Baptist Church: he'd been stealing from the collection plate. Little Roundhead seemed to remember that Reverend Holmes had objected to having such a young boy handle money, but one of the elderly sisters in the congregation reminded the Reverend that Jesus himself had said, "Suffer the little children to come to me."

Still, the Reverend was all over Jeff Ruff like a bloodhound on game, so the boy with the practiced sneer began to ask Reverend Holmes all sorts of questions about God — not because the Reverend knew anything about Him but because Jeff Ruff wanted to get on the Reverend's good side. For a couple of weeks, Jeff Ruff flattered him by pretending an interest in arcane subjects like whether or not the Holy Ghost could help him think pure thoughts. Meanwhile, he had perfected a secret method of palming dollar bills that made it possible to skim a few off the top of the plate while the Reverend wasn't looking. In a couple of months, Jeff Ruff had copped more than thirty dollars, enough to buy a beautiful new bike and a mess of baseball cookies.

"You want yourself a bike? All you got to do is get smart and do the same thing!" Jeff Ruff said. So, sure enough, the very next Sunday, when the Reverend somewhat sarcastically asked, "Is there anybody present who would like to be a member of the church?"—because he asked often and precious few volunteered—Little Roundhead's hand shot up like the tail of a kite in a March wind. Moaning and wailing commenced from the back of the church, causing some in the congregation to turn around to see if Sister Johnson had fallen over again. But the uproar was for him.

"This little boy—son, come on up here and stand next to me—this little boy done put the rest of y'all to shame!" said the Reverend, his face contorted with mock rage. "He is the first from this church to get baptized in over a year!"

Baptized? Who said anything about getting baptized? Little Roundhead tried to bolt from the pulpit, but Reverend Holmes's ham hock-sized hand came down upon his shoulders and pinned him to the ground. "I tell you, the Lord has sent an angel to this congregation in the form of this little boy! And on the twenty-fifth of this month, the Lord will anoint him!" Applause burst from the crowd of worshippers, and the ladies of the congregation rushed to congratulate Mother, kissing her as if she had done something to warrant it. Some of the old men from the congregation stood away from Little Roundhead and pretended to marvel at him. They nodded and stared, seemingly afraid to approach him lest he be caught up in the clouds like the prophet Elijah, and they with him.

Too sophisticated to believe in the Holy Ghost, Little Roundhead had seen his share of Casper cartoons and, because of Grandmama's influence, was all too hip to the machinations of the spirits. No one asked what he thought about God, Christ, baptism, the Devil, the virgin birth. No one asked if he'd even bothered to read the Bible. He would have replied honestly because he had definite opinions about these things. He not only read the Bible, he believed it, although he sometimes wondered whether the Man Upstairs was too busy to be bothered about the problems on earth. He wondered because God had never saved him from a whipping, though he had prayed often and fervently for deliverance.

Little Roundhead was a young free thinker, amused by the lack of spirit in his little church, and more taken with the Reverend Holmes's love of Johnnie Walker Red than his regard for the Almighty. When the Reverend was sober, his preaching reminded Little Roundhead of Bishop Sheen, the father of all televangelists, a ghostly sepulchre of a man. But fired up with alcohol, Reverend Holmes spewed forth sermons that threatened to loosen the floorboards and melt the tar on the roof. On those Sundays, people left the church feeling good about themselves and the sorry old world in which they lived. That's why they turned a blind eye to his drinking—until the day he tried to lift up Sister So-and-So's new dress in the back room.

But that's another story.

When the magic evening came, Little Roundhead and Mother and Father got a ride to the YMCA, because they had no car and Dick, the jitney driver from the A&P, was on a long run. One of the sisters in the congregation swung by in her two-toned Chevrolet and picked up the family. Sister Chauffeur, the folks in the congregation called her, because she liked to honk her car horn as often and as loud as she pleased.

Instead of thinking about the meaning of baptism, Little Roundhead had been dreaming of various ways to decorate his new bike, once he got it. But, when he arrived at the YMCA, later than planned, and heard the combined gospel choirs singing at the tops of their lungs, a sense of dread came over him. As he walked through the doors, some of the spectators pointed at him and whispered in hushed tones. When he saw that they were all dressed in their Sunday-go-to-meeting clothes on a Thursday night, he felt afraid. These people were decked out like they expected Lazarus to come back from the dead.

In the men's locker room, it looked like the Friday night fights as stoop-shouldered black men in white robes paced nervously. An attendant stopped Little Roundhead at the door. "You the kid from the Second Baptist?"

"I guess," Little Roundhead answered.

"Where's your robe?" Little Roundhead shrugged, and the attendant shifted the cigar from one side of his mouth to the other. "I'll get you one—but you better give it back or it comes out of my hide." He gave Roundhead a white terry-cloth robe six sizes too big. "Get your shorts on—and wear a T-shirt if ya wanna."

Once he had changed, the soon-to-be-anointed marched down the corridor toward the pool, into the collective heat of all those people and the sickly smell of chlorine. That and the power of the combined gospel choirs made Roundhead feel as if he were approaching the most holy of holies. By the

time he got to the entrance, his long white robe dragging behind him, he felt dizzy and wanted to throw up. But at times
like these, his fear of embarrassment overcame all other
anxieties and propelled him forward no matter what. This
was a significant character flaw, in his opinion. Throwing up
on cue could be mighty convenient—but he couldn't even
manage to do that right. One of the attendants kept him
back, telling him to wait until the signal came. As he stared
at the people dressed in their finery and wondered why they
weren't at home watching Ozzie and Harriet or something,
he saw himself coasting down the hill on that brand new
J. C. Huffy bike, a nice, bright red one—

"Young brother—step forward, please!" came the com-
mand. Suddenly, every eye fell upon him and, true to his
nature, Little Roundhead strode forward into the water, shed-
ding a robe big enough to cover Muhammad Ali. Reverend
Holmes had planned this moment. As Roundhead walked
down the steps into the pool, the choir grew still and the
crowd hushed. "Friends," said Reverend Holmes, "this here
child is the youngest child ever, in the history of the Baptist
Church in southern Ohio, to dedicate his life to the Lord."
Spontaneous applause broke out among the observers.

"Dedicate his life to the Lord" were the last words Little
Roundhead heard clearly. So chilled by the water and
stricken with panic was he that his knees began to quake and
wouldn't stop. But it was too late for reversals. Still exhorting
and calling upon the Lord, Reverend Holmes grabbed
Little Roundhead's nose, wrapped his massive arms around
the boy's back, and dipped him underneath the water. This
maneuver caught Roundhead by surprise, and he began to
struggle. The others had held their own nostrils while they
were being dipped. But the Reverend tightened his grip

and continued to preach, the sounds now faint to Little Roundhead's submerged ears.

Roundhead had practiced for this moment several times in his own bathtub, but he'd hadn't thought to include terror in the mix of possibilities. Now he was being held under the water at the YMCA by a large, probably drunken man who had his eyes closed, his mouth open, and his mind on God.

Folks later said that they began to worry when tiny air bubbles burst upon the surface of the water, about the time the Reverend Holmes was saying, "We should be thankful that God Almighty has sent an angel into our midst. Now, let us pray." *Now* let us pray?

Then, came the noise—whoosh! Everyone heard it, even Little Roundhead. It was as if a giant whale had let one beneath the water. Up, up, up came the startled boy child, borne on an air bubble, up as if vomited out of the mouth of a big fish. The bubble propelled the boy out of the arms of Reverend Holmes, and the dazzled crowd gasped with relief and awe at the sight of Roundhead popping out of the water, sucking air.

For years, folks talked of Little Roundhead's submersion the way people do when they have seen something wonderful that they did not fully understand. Some said it was a divine mystery how the boy was saved from drowning. A few elderly ones of the congregation swore they saw the Holy Ghost swimming down there with Little Roundhead on the evening of his deliverance. Like the children of Abraham, he had been marked by that spirit, they said, and would lead a charmed life. Reverend Holmes declared the baptism a miracle and promptly invited himself over for Sunday dinner.

Little Roundhead wasn't confused. He understood perfectly what had happened to him. He knew what force it was that saved him from an evil end and spared his dear mother untold grief. He knew because try as he might the following Sunday, he could not bring himself to pilfer the congregation's crumpled, hard-earned dollar bills. J. C. Huffy would just have to wait for another day, another year.

Because Little Roundhead knew, with a knowledge that surpassed all understanding, that even if Reverend Holmes was a tired old drunkard, even if Jeff Ruff was a crook, even if the congregation was weak and sinful — even if the church itself was completely devoid of spirit — God Himself was astonishingly, everlastingly alive.

Jesus Wept

Little Roundhead stood poised on a hill, a miniature boulder trembling in his hand, rage coursing through his body like an electric current. Beneath him, rolling waves of heat bounced off the fortresslike headquarters of the Fourth Police Precinct, and Rubel's German bakery belched forth pumpernickel smoke from its stack the way it always did. A great chasm had just opened beneath Roundhead's feet and threatened to swallow him whole. But the natural world showed no sign of cataclysm. All was calm, peaceful.

He had been taught to respect his elders. He had come of age when the Good Book was still read and appreciated as the Word of God, not a history text. The sacred teachings were passed down to him in bite-sized chunks, so that by the time he turned ten, he knew just enough to be dangerous. He knew, for example, that "Jesus wept" was the shortest verse in the Bible, although the idea of the Son of God weeping didn't make sense to him.

A few weeks before he found himself looking down upon

the police precinct station with a stone in his hand, Little Roundhead solved the mystery of the weeping savior, or so he thought. "Dear Jesus," he asked one night underneath his bed covers, "Why does my father fight with my mama like that? She's so little . . ." In the mournful silence that followed, Little Roundhead lifted his eyes toward the heavens and waited for an answer. He waited a long time and then, suddenly, the answer came: outside, it began to rain.

To a child like Roundhead—a mystically devout child who believed in his heart that God was his real father—an answer like that could bring a smile even in the midst of tears. Dizzied by the sheer possibility for goodness in himself and his neighbors, Roundhead felt in his bones the startling electric connection that today we call spirit. His skin and features took in the natural elements as if he owned them, so that all things made and existing resounded within his body, echoing from some deep-heart place he kept locked away, safe from the whims of foreign gods and goddesses.

The rain was a sign to Little Roundhead that Jesus wept not once, but for all time and for all of us. That night he understood that sadness and suffering are part of life, a part of nature itself, and that we needn't be imprisoned by them. Indeed, sadness, like rain, always brings forth joy, like flowers, if we can only survive to see it blossom. These lessons he took from the natural elements. But there was much more to learn.

Unnatural elements, like the rage of his father, shook him to his core. He didn't know how it had started or when, but from as far back as Little Roundhead could remember, Father had been angry. At the dinner table, the Old Man spoke bitterly about the white man for whom he worked, a man called Red.

"That cracker's always on me, telling me what to do!" he would shout. There were times when the Old Man would burst through the door after a day at work, take off his belt, and begin to whip anyone who moved. But the most frightening times were the days when he said nothing to anyone. On those days, the Old Man never stopped working. Work was a tonic in his mind and he drank deeply of it, forcing all around him to imbibe. He came home, peeled off his clothing, and silently dressed in trousers and a T-shirt, readying himself for a second shift in the backyard, the kitchen, the cellar. He sawed, hammered, mixed and laid cement until the natural light faded and fatigue overcame him. If anything went wrong, the anger would flash behind his eyes like lightning.

"C'mon out here, boy! I got something for you to do!" he would bark. If Roundhead moved slowly, because his little mind might be elsewhere at any given moment, a sharp slap across the face got his attention. A knuckle sandwich. A kick in the pants. A whipping with a green switch, freshly peeled from a tree, or with the broad belt Father wore to hold up his pants. These were the signposts of communication between Little Roundhead and the Old Man.

"Don't let him come back, please," Little Roundhead sometimes prayed, holding his little sister, when the Old Man left. Picklehead, normally so shy she had been known to jump at the sight of her own shadow, would chime in brightly, "Maybe his bus will go over the cliff in Eden Park!" For a moment, Roundhead would try to imagine the number 49 bus careening into the Eden Park reservoir, killing all aboard, but even then it was clear that the Old Man was a terrifying, immutable force. Trying to kill him would be like trying to kill a fortress.

As the boy grew older, the fear gradually began to be replaced by indignation, and the indignation by cold, hard anger. Once, when Father beat him for betting fifty cents on a football game, Mother intervened and took the brunt of strong blows just long enough to distract the Old Man and make him forget why he was whipping Little Roundhead in the first place.

When the fight became theirs and theirs alone, as it often did, Roundhead's misery increased tenfold. Better that he be whipped than Mother. It was then that he began to find his maleness, his own blinding fury. It was then that he began, stupidly, to plant his young body between the two people he loved most on earth, hoping to make them stop it, pushing them back from each other and the brink of chaos, toward a time when they must have loved better and more completely than this. But somehow, even as he pushed, he knew it wouldn't help. Once the anger began, the Old Man didn't see him, didn't see anyone, and the void of his gaze became a cavernous pit of blinding rage.

In the midst of one of these interventions, Father turned on Little Roundhead and grabbed him by the throat, lifting him off the ground in his anger. Like a shark in a feeding frenzy, he shook the boy and threw him across the room while Mother pleaded with him to stop. This time, Little Roundhead took off on a dead run out the door and up the street to Highland Avenue. The colors and sounds of the hot summer street all blended together as he put one foot in front of the other. He thought of running to Grandmama's house, but that was too far away. He was certain that Mother would be dead by the time he returned.

The Fourth Police Precinct house stood at the southwest end of Avondale, a neighborhood near Corryville that had once been entirely German. Now only the poorest of the poor lived in the few ugly homes that dotted the area, where a lumberyard and train station nearly collided with Rubel's bakery. Roundhead had never before entered a police station, but not even the imposing bars that covered its windows could deter him.

The reddish dust of the street covered his sweat-drenched face, and he must have looked like a madman when he entered and spoke to the staff sergeant.

"Come quick!" Little Roundhead gasped. "My daddy's killing my mother!"

The staff sergeant, a black man, pushed his white hat back and eyed Little Roundhead with skepticism. "Killing her? What'd she do?"

"She didn't do nothing!" He shook his head. "He's beating her up! You gotta stop him!"

The staff sergeant chuckled. "That's between your daddy and your momma, son," said the man. "We can't do nothing about that."

"You don't understand," shouted Little Roundhead, causing the other officers to stop and stare. "He's hurting her!"

The officer paused and looked up again from his paperwork. "You go on home, son," he said. And then, after another pause, he looked down on the sweaty little boy and said, "Someday soon, when you grow up to be a man, you'll understand." Little Roundhead backed away, staring at the pious white-shirted officers in utter disbelief.

Outside now, his mind racing, he hyperventilated and staggered as if he were drunk, back up the hill the way he came. But his anger soon righted him. The injustice of it carried him to a place overlooking the precinct house, high above it, where he stood staring, weeping, gasping for breath. So these were the police. The peacekeepers. Those who swore to protect and serve. The men behind the badges. Our friends.

Little Roundhead bent down and grasped a large, round rock, smooth as a puppy's nose. He hesitated. No one could see him. Yelling, he dipped back and launched the rock high in the air, falling backward as he did so, tripping and tumbling down the gravelly hill into the lumberyard. The rough-edged stones felt good as they cut and nicked him. They felt good because now he was one of them. A stone. Hardened by time and circumstance. Made for throwing.

Hurtling alone through space and time, the rock hit the window instead of the thick steel bars. Sharp, shattering chimes of glass rang out in crazy celebration of his manhood. But these bells of sand quickly gave way to an urgent, pulsating alarm. Little Roundhead, surprised and overjoyed at first, jumped up from the stone pile confused.

Yes, he was now a warrior-man. But in becoming that which he had avoided his entire young life, he felt unnatural. Provoked by fear, he had struck back out of some ancient instinct to conceal his true emotion—an overwhelming sadness so deep it threatened to envelop him in permanent grief. In that moment, Little Roundhead understood the true nature of Father's rage and that of the whole testosterone-drenched world. He understood the uneasy alliance of the rock and the hard place, the truth and falsity that form the craggy seat of manhood. This was why Jesus wept—He wept to keep from killing somebody. This was why weeping was good.

Little Roundhead understood. And he ran.

The Fight

Growing up in a neighborhood where violence was the shadow child of rage, Roundhead despaired of ever finding true peace. Knifings, beatings, dogfights, glue sniffing, alcohol abuse, rapes, and occasionally shootings were commonplace. No one called this "violence" in the early 1960s. It was just "the way it is." Random cruelty hung in the air: boys molesting girls, fights taking place atop the monkey bars, older boys beating younger ones for twenty-five cents—their lunch money.

"You gonna have to learn to fight, that's all there is to it," Little Roundhead's next-door neighbor, Clifford, counseled one spring morning. "If you don't, you gonna get your head knocked clean offa your body," he said, fixing Roundhead with a stern stare.

"But I don't wanna fight," Little Roundhead protested. "What good's it gonna do?"

"You gotta protect yourself, fool!" Clifford yelled. "Or you gonna end up dead!"

Well, at least he knew he had choices. Since he'd been sexually molested and had told the police, the whole neighborhood had turned against him. He fought as best he could, running away much of the time, often coming home with a bloodied nose. Sometimes dead seemed like the best alternative.

One boy in particular truly hated Little Roundhead, an older boy named Paul Davis. For a total of twenty consecutive school days, Paul beat up Little Roundhead on the way to school, and Roundhead, technically under school protection because he'd been molested, reported the beatings to the principal, as ordered. Each day, Paul was given an additional swat with a wooden paddle for beating Little Roundhead, beginning with twenty. At the thirty mark, the number of swats was doubled, to sixty. All of this was done in front of Little Roundhead to humiliate Paul and show him the error of his ways.

But Paul continued to harass Little Roundhead despite the paddling. This was where the boy began to see that just as he had been born a pacifist, some people came out of the chute looking for a fight. He had done his Christian duty and turned the other cheek as often as he could. It was time to fight back. Roundhead told Clifford he was ready. Clifford chuckled. "You ain't ready by a long shot," he said. "You need training."

Clifford ran Little Roundhead ragged, up and down stairs, jumping rope, riding bicycles, doing push-ups, and learning to "stick and move." Together, they took a field trip to the YMCA and studied the moves of real boxers, palookas who knew the sweet science better than they knew their own names. As the day approached, Roundhead began to feel the muscles in his little arms bulging through his shirt. His legs took on the shape and proportion of a man's, and tiny hairs sprouted on his chest and chin.

The fateful Saturday came all too quickly. Roundhead still hoped to avoid a fight. In his mind's eye, he saw himself sitting down in the grass and talking to Paul, trying to reason with him. They didn't need to be enemies. Why couldn't they be friends? Instinctively, Roundhead knew why: because although they shared the same skin color and lived only three blocks apart, they were from different worlds. Paul's parents seemed not to care about their children. They let them run through the neighborhood like orphans, and soon they became like wild dogs. All the rage those boys felt at being abandoned doubled back on the neighborhood and took its toll on those who chose to live differently. It was the way of the world.

The ragged little boys and older hustlers wearing do rags to protect their processed hair gathered in the park along with the winos, the weirdos, and the scraggly girls who hung out hoping to be noticed by the very boys who would later come to hate them. As Roundhead stretched his limbs against an oak tree, Clifford barked last-minute instructions. "You gotta start fast—hit him hard, like you hit that flour bag the other day, and he won't never get up!" But Little Roundhead was only half listening. He had left his body to fly high overhead and look down at the fiasco of twenty to thirty Negroes surrounding two young boys determined to maim each other. He simply could not believe this was happening to him.

"Who gotta watch with a second hand?" Clifford asked. Several boys stepped forward and opened their jackets, displaying their wares. He borrowed Tony's Timex. As the makeshift bell, a large oatmeal pot, rang out the start of round one, Roundhead found himself stuck to the oak tree.

"I don't wanna! No! I don't wanna!" he shouted, fear, shame, and shyness all surging through his body at the same time. The watching boys roared with laughter as Clifford shook the little beanhead by his shoulders. "What you afraid of?" Clifford demanded.

Confused, Roundhead answered, "I don't wanna die!" to which Clifford replied, "It ain't your time to die—you said so yourself—remember?"

That's right—people had tried to kill him before and failed. Even a drunken Reverend Holmes hadn't been able to drown him during his baptism. Why was he worried about puny little Paul Davis? A surge of adrenaline caught Roundhead, spun him around, and catapulted him to the middle of the ring, where he swung wildly, missing everything. Paul kicked him in the back and sent Roundhead sprawling. But kicking was against the rules, and this wanton violation fortified the little boy even more. He turned around and let go a combination left-left-right that caught Paul in the face and midsection. Stunned, the older boy dropped his guard just long enough to allow Roundhead to launch a haymaker that caught him dead center in his forehead.

That mighty blow could have crushed Paul Davis's skull or broken Roundhead's hand. But as Paul collapsed, Roundhead didn't feel a thing. He had lost all consciousness of his own body and stood over his fallen opponent howling like a rabid dog. "Now who's bad! Now who's bad! Now who's bad!"

Money changed hands in a heartbeat as the stunned crowd surged toward Little Roundhead in amazement, shouting in disbelief. Clifford picked up the dazed fighter and carried him on his shoulders up the street away from the rabble.

Overcome by excitement, Roundhead could scarcely breathe. As Clifford ran out to tell the world what had happened, Little Roundhead, alone now in Clifford's basement, exhausted, knew that the long hard battle had just begun. Now he would become a target for every intemperate or insane boy in the city, boys with little better to do than spend a quarter on bus fare to fight someone they didn't even know.

In that instant he saw the whole thing: Negroes half-killing each other because they were angry — angry because they were poor and powerless. Fighting each other instead of fighting the real enemies, ignorance and prejudice. Fighting to win a commodity more scarce than gold in his community—self-esteem. Like a trophy that rotated from one winner to the next, those who had it held onto it for dear life, while those who lacked it would do anything to gain it.

He saw it all but despaired of ever making anyone understand. All he had were words, and what good were words against brass knuckles, knives, and guns? Words—the music of the true and living spirit that dwelt above the clouds. But how could they be made vital to those who lived with daily abuse and neglect? Roundhead called to that spirit silently, beseeching it to mold him, shape him. And he saw then that the only way out was to make his people not only hear his words but also feel their own lifeblood pounding within them.

The World Widens

Baseball

Cincinnati took pride in many things, including such mundane items as its impressive chili, its selection of beers, and its conservative Republican traditions. But pride in the Cincinnati Reds baseball team surpassed even these and, remarkably, extended from the late ninteenth century clear into the ignominious Marge Schott era. Cincinnati had been the cradle of professional baseball. The 1919 team was the beneficiary of the Black Sox scandal, which awarded the World Series to the Reds for the first time. The hometown boys won the National League pennant back-to-back in 1939 and 1940, and folks began to talk about a dynasty. But it was just talk.

By the time Roundhead came on the scene in 1951, the color barrier had been shattered by Jackie Robinson, but the color issue still dominated conversation. That's because those who ruled baseball feared black players. Men like Kenesaw Mountain Landis, Connie Mack, and John MacGraw were steeped in racist beliefs that they never outgrew. They figured if black players were allowed into the major leagues, white kids might want to grow up to be like them. Even worse, white women might be attracted to these players, and where would that leave the white man? This was the subtext beneath the other explanations, the chief reason why Branch Rickey picked a married college graduate to be the first colored baseball star.

Of course, while Negroes were admonished to mind their p's and q's if they ever hoped to get into the major leagues, white ballplayers like Ty Cobb, Babe Ruth, Mickey Cochrane, Mickey Mantle, and the infamous Dean Brothers could do whatever they wanted. When they acted like fools, people called it—oddly enough—colorful.

A couple of the Reds' greatest stars in the 1950s and 1960s—the immortal Frank Robinson and Vada Pinson—were more than just ballplayers to Little Roundhead. He looked up to them as genuine heroes whose example of excellence inspired his own derring-do. Robinson in particular represented the second generation of Negro players, and his militant antidiscrimination stance at the ballpark made many colored people see that they could be anything they wanted—if they were prepared to demand it.

Roundhead and his friends took a long look at the team that dominated the game in the 1950s, the Yankees, and rejected them out of hand. They were a throwback to segregated baseball, a largely white team, with the exception of Elston Howard, who proved the rule. To be a big-time Yankee player, you had to be white and preferably Italian. All anyone heard about were Babe Ruth, Lou Gehrig, Joe DiMaggio, Billy Martin, Whitey Ford, Mickey Mantle, Roger Maris, and the famous Yankee pinstripes. Great players all, and Roundhead admired their abilities. But even as a young boy, he saw through the media hype and felt betrayed by the racial chauvinism of the Yankees.

The moment the first black man stepped on a baseball field, he changed the game. You could call it blackball. Roundhead had seen it played at the rec center, where men with cast-iron bodies ripped the tar out of the ball and ran faster than the professionals. Guys from the neighborhood—truck drivers, waiters, security guards—played the game with lightning speed and absolute abandon. It was about stealing home, taking that extra base, throwing your body as well as the ball. It was about style. Mostly, that kind of magic occurred on the playgrounds and in the National League. American League baseball bored Roundhead to tears. The umpires called high strikes, and the players were so slow the Junior Circuit seemed to be stuck in time.

On opening day of the baseball season in Cincinnati, the city celebrated with a massive downtown parade that had the feel of a rite of spring, a fertility ritual. If you owned a ticket to the game, you could skip school, and even if you didn't it was presumed that everyone's eyes would be glued to the TV set or that they would be listening to Waite Hoyt on radio. The games meant so much to Roundhead and his family that no one wanted to miss even the first pitch of the season, much less the game itself. It was as if the whole city were starting over again, and baseball, with its fresh dirt and well-manicured field, provided the proper setting for forgiveness of sins.

More than just a national pastime, baseball was Cincinnati's game, and thus it was also Roundhead's. Long before he ever picked up a baseball or threw a high hard one or slid into home plate, Roundhead would sit on his father's lap wearing a Cincinnati Reds cap and holding a tiny, infant-sized bat. Father would say "Swing!" as the pitcher threw the ball on TV, and Roundhead would swing so hard his little body would twist nearly in two. This made Father and Mother crack up laughing and put Roundhead in the same league as all those other boys and girls in Cincinnati who wanted, desperately, for at least ten years, to be nothing other than ballplayers.

Gradually, as he grew older, Roundhead began to gain weight, so that his skin became puffy and his stomach protruded a little over his pants. Baby fat, Mother called it. Others called it obesity, plain and simple, which hurt Little Roundhead's feelings. It took a lot to be considered fat in those days. Good-looking people always carried a little extra weight in the Negro community—in case of famine, natural disaster, or unwarranted arrest. Besides, nobody with a grandmama could get away with being skinny.

People did what were called calisthenics—organized exercise—to get in shape. A he-man named Jack LaLane had a morning television show aimed at idle women who wanted to lose weight. You could see from watching the show that LaLane might have cared a little bit about the audience, but he did the show for himself because it made him feel good.

There were other, more exciting ways of getting in shape. Roundhead played as often as he could but not in any organized way until Rodney McDowell, his neighbor, said to him one day, "I'm playing baseball with a team called the Gibson Greeting Cardinals. Wanna come?" The Gibson Greeting Card Company, located out in the white suburbs, was the kind of institution that seldom reached into the Negro community. They must have figured that Negroes didn't buy greeting cards, because Roundhead had never heard of them.

"How far from home do we have to go?" Roundhead asked.

"Don't worry about it. You just get on the bus with me."

"How much does it cost?" Roundhead inquired.

"Don't cost nothing. The coach will pay the bus fare. Just get on the bus. I thought you wanted to play ball?"

"Yeah, I do," said Roundhead. "I just want to know the details."

They went together the following week and, on the bus ride out, Roundhead saw parts of Cincinnati he never knew existed. Beautiful homes, landscaped gardens, large shopping malls. If the team was anything like these neighborhoods, he would enjoy baseball immensely.

"Let's see if you can hit the glove, son," said the coach to Little Roundhead. He wore a slightly bemused look on his moon-shaped face, for Roundhead was not an impressive physical specimen, and this was his first organized baseball practice. But that didn't stop the boy from winding up like Bob Gibson and firing a fastball into the coach's mitt. The coach dropped the glove and squeezed his hand in pain.

"Who the hell is this kid?" he mumbled to the assistant coach. "He's gotta have played ball somewhere." All those games of strikeout in the sideyard had begun to pay off.

The season had begun two weeks earlier, and now the Gibson Greeting Cardinals were 0-2, having lost to the other patsies in the league by the ten-run rule. This rule often saved time and anguish by declaring that if, by the end of a certain inning, a team was ahead by ten runs, they won the game. The Cardinals badly needed new blood, so the coach asked his star pitcher, Rodney, to bring one or two Negro boys from the neighborhood with him when he came the next week. Sure, he'd pay the bus fare, he said. So Rodney delivered Roundhead.

The team was all Jewish except for Rodney, and the neighborhoods where the games were played were far, far away from Roundhead's Corryville address. But the suburban league offered something no local league could deliver—a midseason all-star game, complete with a most valuable player trophy. Newspapers actually printed the box scores from the games and often published photos. This promise of esteem made Roundhead long to make his mark so he could start to feel that he belonged somewhere, anywhere.

On a hot summer evening the Gibson Greeting Cardinals played a little catch, a little pepper, a little situation ball, worked on hitting the cutoff man—"not literally," the coach had to explain. Then they took a little batting practice, and the new kid, Little Roundhead, got honors.

"You know how to hold a bat, don't you?" shouted the coach, who saw that Roundhead had forgotten to turn the sweet spot around so the timber wouldn't break. The kids all chuckled at the coach's remark, but Roundhead took offense.

"What you mean, do I know how to hold a bat?" he asked, backing out of the batter's box, staring at the coach. His anger boiled up more quickly than it used to.

"I'll show you how I hold a bat," said Little Roundhead, and he sent the next pitch sailing out to left center field near the railroad tracks.

The boys looked at Roundhead, then looked at the ball, then looked back at Roundhead. "Someone hustle that ball," said the coach nervously. "We can't afford to lose any more this year."

"Who's he?" one of the kids asked. "Is he going to play for us?"

Roundhead bent down over the plate in anticipation of the next pitch. "Cracka" went the ball, screaming down the left field line. One of the parents in the stands whistled and took off his cap. Roundhead loved the sound the ball made when he hit it just right: "cracka" was how he felt about the boys who had snubbed him when he first came to practice. "Cracka" was his answer to the coach's insulting question about the bat. Next pitch — "cracka," back across the mound like a bullet toward the coach, who improvised a cha-cha getting out of the way. It was a message hit, and the coach knew it. But instead of being angry, he paused calmly and said, "You got a lot of venom in you, don't you, little man?"

The assistant coach pulled Roundhead out of the batter's box. "We need you to sign this contract," he said. The piece of paper, emblazoned with an American flag and the Knothole League logo at the top, said Roundhead could play baseball with the Gibson Greeting Cardinals but no one else that season. Instinctively, he began to bargain. What could he finagle for giving up his right to play elsewhere?

"You'll be playing real baseball," the assistant coach said, "wearing a real uniform. Plus, we get everybody a soda pop and chips after every game." That sounded good to Roundhead, but he had something else in mind.

"You know, it costs us twenty-five cents to get out here and twenty-five cents to get back."

The assistant coach nodded. "We'll take care of that. We know your family doesn't have a car."

Roundhead signed the piece of paper because the chance to play real baseball, as the coach had put it, was too sweet to turn down. The diamond had real bases, real grass, and a sanded infield. Where he came from, the baseball field had at least one rock for a bag, and you couldn't tell where the infield ended and the outfield began.

On Saturday morning, Roundhead woke up at six, so excited was he at the prospect of playing. Meanwhile, Father had decided he wanted to see his boy play. It was a natural enough instinct. Father had taught Little Roundhead how to throw a ball very early in life. He had taken him to a couple of games at Crosley Field, where they'd sat in the bleachers together and watched their heroes play. But Father was so critical of anything Roundhead did, it made the boy nervous to perform in front of him.

To make matters worse, once they got to the field, the coach said that Roundhead's uniform hadn't come in yet. He had worn a pair of Harry Belafonte calypso pants and a striped shirt, intending to change in the park restroom. He would look ridiculous playing baseball in this kind of outfit in front of all those rich people. Then the coach told him he would not be the starting pitcher, and his heart sank even further.

So Little Roundhead rode the bench with the scrubs — inquisitive kids, all destined to be doctors or dentists. As he sat there, his blood pressure rising higher and higher at the prospect of missing the whole game, a wave of shame came over him. Why had he assumed he could start in his first game, anyway? And hadn't he ruined the whole thing himself by showing up in those ridiculous clothes? He was dressed for a limbo party, not a game.

As he looked around, nothing but white faces and bermuda shorts, gabardine slacks, madras shirts, penny loafers, sandals, and the painted toes of certain ladies greeted him from the gallery. The outfits were casual but new. There wasn't a single hole in anyone's shirt or pants that he could see. Then it occurred to him that these people were decked out for church, not baseball. In fact, so many of them argued with the umpire over every call that the game felt churchlike to Roundhead. Their responses to the umpire were like those of the congregation when the preacher said something powerful and the brothers and sisters responded with "Amen" or "Preach on."

Out here, in the synagogue of baseball, when the preacher said "Strike" or "Safe!" the congregation moaned and offered him its glasses. They stood up and yelled with passionate animation, shaking the fence, screaming disapproval. Some even directed the game itself.

"Barry! You're playing way too shallow! Come in a little! This kid's no hitter up here at the plate." Yes, they even made comments about the players, the ten-year-olds, many of whom came into the batter's box shaking like a leaf.

The coach's son, Bobby, had been the starting pitcher and managed to throw the ball over the plate enough times to keep the score close. Although Roundhead burned inside because he hadn't played, what really hurt him was that they were losing. The Gibson Greeting Cardinals were behind two to one in the last inning—incredibly low numbers for a game in which kids often scored on infield hits and overthrows.

Who did the coach call on to pinch hit in the last inning but the boy in the calypso pants? If Roundhead could have found a hole to crawl into, he would have. Burning from the insults he expected from the crowd, he felt angry and nervous. But that didn't last long. He selected the largest bat he could find, took a few practice swings in the dugout so no one could see him, then waited as the first batter struck out before walking to the plate. He heard the mumbles of the crowd, the laughter, but most of all he heard Father say, "It's about time! That's my son!" And the crowd settled down.

On the first pitch, Roundhead swung so hard he hit himself in the foot with the bat and hobbled away from the plate. Only years later would he understand the term Achilles' heel, but on this day he lived out its meaning. On the next pitch — cracka! — Roundhead drove the ball a country mile to dead center, far over the head of the center fielder, who was so awed by the hit that he turned and watched it sail over the railroad tracks. The opposing coach turned apoplectic.

"Get the ball! Get the ball!"

There were no automatic homers in this league. Players had to leg it out. As the ball rolled across the railroad cinders, Roundhead chugged to first base and turned on the afterburners. By the time he got to second base, the adrenaline had tired him out, and the stupid calypso pants had begun to loosen and threatened to fall. He headed for third, holding his pants tightly, breathing like an out-of-shape workhorse. His teammates shouted encouragement, waved him on, but halfway to third, fatigue took over and he could barely lift his legs any longer. Still, he sucked it in and turned around third headed for home, determined to win the game.

As the sound of a freight train echoed from the outfield, Roundhead's wide turn at third scattered the opposing team's bench players, who saw their lives pass before their very eyes. He started to dream about being a hero, about an extra soda pop and a second bag of chips. By the time he came back to earth again, the catcher already had the ball. He planted himself in front of the plate as he'd been told to do, but the sheer terror on that little boy's face said that he wished to God he'd gone fishing that day. The catcher had freckles, every one of which Roundhead could see as he chugged into home with everyone yelling, "Slide! Slide! Slide!!!"

Roundhead hit the dirt, but he was only three-quarters of the way home, and he plowed into the ground like a John Deere, well away from home plate. Greatly relieved, the little boy in the catcher's outfit gingerly applied the tag.

"You're out!" yelled the umpire. A thousand voices moaned in disappointment. There was no question about the call. The only question was how Roundhead could avoid collapsing in shame and humiliation, not to mention exhaustion.

On the bus ride home, Roundhead could barely talk. The Old Man criticized him, saying he'd taught Roundhead better than that.

"You shoulda bowled over that little Irish catcher 'cause he was scared of you and woulda dropped the ball. I can't believe it. Hit the ball that far and don't score." The Old Man shook his head. When they got home, Roundhead was too ashamed to go inside and face his mother.

"Well, how'd he do?" Mother asked the Old Man, whose voice went up an entire octave when he said, "You shoulda seen how far the boy hit that ball! He played one hell of a game, for it being his first time out."

The Old Man didn't say this to Roundhead, and he didn't know Roundhead was within earshot. As the little beanhead listened, he couldn't help himself. The edge of his lips quivered, like they didn't want to do it. But in the end he smiled and shook his head at what he had done on the very first day he ever played real baseball.

Work

> The heights by great men reached and kept
> Were not attained by sudden flight,
> But they, while their companions slept,
> Were toiling upward in the night.
> *Henry Wadsworth Longfellow*

The most constant thing in Little Roundhead's life, modeled by both Father and Mother, was the exchange of time and labor for capital called work. Work drove the entire household, and Roundhead was in the thick of it. Father finally settled at the Board of Education, where he became a janitor and worked long hours. Later, on the weekends, he massaged the backs of rich people at the Jewish Community Center to make even more money for his family. Mother worked several different shifts as a licensed practical nurse on her way to becoming a private-duty nurse.

Roundhead studied his parents and came away in awe. They worked so hard at times it made him wonder if life was worth the sheer physical expenditure of all that energy on behalf of something that seemed unconnected to their hearts. Father seemed to hate his work, but it was difficult to know because he seldom spoke of it in plain, forthright words. His fatigue at the end of the day didn't stop him from tossing a ball with his son, who loved the challenge of a good game of strikeout. The Old Man always beat him at this game, because he didn't have the same ego needs as Little Roundhead. Their strikeout encounters became enormous struggles to Roundhead, who sought some affirmation of his manhood from challenges like these. He wanted to win every game to prove that he was born with the same masculine stuff as Father and would some day surpass him.

There were always chores to do. Chores were tasks assigned by parents to their children that carried with them several messages: "You live here, you eat here—you work here"; "Life is hard and you'd better get used to it"; "If you can't take out the garbage on time, you can't get up and go to work on time"; and, finally, "Ain't nobody gonna give you nothing you don't work for."

At first, Roundhead believed that work might just be optional if a person could figure out how to avoid it. Why work all day when there were so many wonderful things to discover in the natural world? Why worry about money when the neighborhood had pop and beer bottles lying on the ground, waiting to be redeemed? Even the local cleaners would pay a dime for a bundle of usable hangers. So why work?

The answer came up out of the ground one evening as Roundhead and Father surveyed their handicraft, a new concrete slab that ran the length of the side yard. The two of them had slaved for several days over this installation. They broke up rocks with sledgehammers in what seemed to Roundhead to be the kind of futile, spirit-breaking, back-aching work suited only to convicts. But gradually, under Father's tutelage, he began to see the point. They mixed the rock with sand and something called Sakrete, using a hoe and just the right amount of water. Father measured the area meticulously and roped it off, then used the saw to cut two-by-fours to block off the length of the side yard. This took several days of work after school and on weekends, when Roundhead normally would have preferred to be daydreaming or playing in the park.

Roundhead dared not complain because Father wouldn't stand for it. But still, the boy wasn't quite ready to end his childhood so early and struggled against being dragged into the adult world under such harsh circumstances. As a result, Roundhead often worked slowly, unconscious of what he was doing.

"Hey, boy! Watch what you doing there!" Father would call out, frowning. Roundhead typically would stop and say, "What *am* I doing?" which provoked anger and revulsion from the Old Man. Sometimes this response would spring Roundhead from his duties as Father pushed him aside and said, "You ain't good for nothing, you know that?" He had heard this statement so many times before it didn't settle inside him now as it once did. He took it as Father's frustration that he didn't have a son who was just like him in every way, a son who cared about concrete and woodworking. Inside, Father seethed constantly, as if no one was ever good enough for him. It was his way, and he did it to everyone in the family.

But the side-yard project became something of an epiphany to Little Roundhead. After all the rock crushing and mixing and measuring and sifting that seemed so futile, Father poured the smooth new concrete and began to pack it into place, so that it filled the areas he had carefully measured. Then he took a smoothing tool and gently rolled the concrete mixture back and forth, until it began to thin out in certain places and flowed easily within the boxed areas. He used his tools with the finesse of a trained bricklayer, but Father had no training—he was simply a genius when it came to working with his hands.

They covered the area for several days, then removed the tarpaulin. Beneath it, the new sidewalk glowed from the love and care Father had given it, and Roundhead surveyed the work with a kind of personal pride. Father didn't say anything except "Looks pretty good," but as they stood there together admiring it, Roundhead felt a closeness that had all too often eluded them. Work, he began to see, was the key to progress and, perhaps, a new relationship with Father. Without work, people would be doomed to live in the past, never attaining new goals, achieving new victories, moving ahead. Work created satisfaction, even if it paid not a single red cent. Work carried its own rewards: pride in the finished product, victory over fatigue, mastery of skills and tools, and the camaraderie of collaboration.

Roundhead seldom worked with Mother, but he felt that her passion for it equaled Father's. In fact, this was one of the few ways in which Mother and Father seemed perfectly matched. Mother could work back-to-back eight-hour nursing shifts and still be loving to her family. After coming home, tired but cheerful, she would cook and clean the same as any other mother, and aside from being lost in thought from time to time like Roundhead, she was always ready to help her children with any problem.

By the time Roundhead turned ten, he had four siblings: Picklehead, Featherhead, Ohio State-head, and Hardhead, Roundhead's only brother. Later, the final child, Pinhead, came into the world, and somebody decided that they'd had enough. Mother worked right up until the day she went into the hospital to deliver her babies. Economic necessity drove her to work. She'd been trained to help people, and among those she helped by contributing her income was her family. But she might as easily have concluded that unrelenting work, six children, and a constantly critical husband were too much to deal with.

Mother's attitude toward the outside world came from

Grandmama, who knew how to save money, how to find bargains at department stores, and how to deal with unruly folks of all kinds. She owned several pieces of rental property and had a lawyer named Mebs whom she called whenever she needed him. Mother was just as industrious in her own way. She taught Roundhead to read the want ads in the newspaper every week because "You never can tell when you might find something better."

Something better. That's why Father and Mother worked so hard. Father told Roundhead that if he wanted to have his own money, he needed to look for a job.

"You can start by mowing people's lawns like some of the other boys do," Father said. "See how much you can make doing that."

At fifty cents a lawn, he'd have to cut a lot of grass with that old push mower to get much spending money. He had a better idea: why not work in the barbershop up the street? Bishop Early's barbershop? And why not sell the *Call and Post*, the newspaper for the Negro community? Soon after he became a paperboy, Roundhead went to Bishop Early, who seemed amused and proud of the boy. "I could use somebody to sweep up around here," he said, "but only on Saturdays. We closed on the Lord's day."

Roundhead took the job and thanked him, wondering if he had done the right thing. It was only a weekend job. But once he got there, he had another thought: why not shine the shoes of the patrons in the barbershop and increase his income?

Bishop Early eyed Roundhead dubiously.

"What makes you think people want to get a shoe shine while they're getting their hair cut?" he asked skeptically.

"They have to think about two things at once and that ain't no good."

"The way I look at it," said Roundhead, "they'll have two different reasons for coming into the shop. If they don't want a haircut they can come in for a shine. And vice versa."

"I don't know." Bishop Early clucked his tongue. "You can try it this Saturday and we'll see if it works. If it don't . . ."

Not only did it work, but several patrons praised Bishop Early for being so thoughtful and for providing the service. Roundhead shined nine pairs of shoes that day and could have shined more if he hadn't run out of polish. He'd been working with half-empty tins of brown, black, and clear polish, thinking he might not get much business. He made at least twenty-five cents on every shine, plus a few dimes and nickels in tips. Bishop Early paid him a dollar an hour to clean up, dust patrons off after a haircut, shake the bib, and yell "Next!" On a good day he made ten dollars from his duties at Bishop Early's shop and two or three dollars from selling newspapers and shining shoes.

As he began to understand selling, Roundhead realized that making money was about building relationships with people. Giving them what they wanted when they wanted it usually spurred extra tips and high praise. Bishop Early began to listen to the boy as he made new suggestions.

"Why don't you let me set up a couple of newspaper stands in here, Bishop?" Roundhead asked.

"What for? We get the newspaper."

"Yeah, that's the *Enquirer*. I'm talking about the *Call and Post* and the *Cincinnati Herald*, the Negro papers. I bet if we put some of them in here, convenient for the customer, we'd sell 'em to people waiting on haircuts."

"I don't know," clucked Bishop Early. "What's in it for me, partner?"

"I'll give you half of what I earn—three cents a paper," said Roundhead.

"Three cents?!" Bishop Early recoiled. "That's all you make offa selling them papers? They oughta be ashamed of themselves. That ain't hardly nothing!"

"I make six cents. What I'm saying is, I'll give you half. That's three cents." To Roundhead, six cents was sufficient for selling a paper that he had no hand in creating.

"Boy, keep your little ole three cents. Bring ten copies of the papers next week, and we'll see how they do." Bishop Early paused and grinned. "You must have a fever all the time, boy."

"A fever?"

"'Cause you don't never stop thinking!"

The next Saturday, Roundhead created a nearly illegible cardboard sign advertising the papers. He sold out that morning. Some patrons even bought both papers for thirty-five cents, amazing Roundhead. That evening, as Roundhead finished sweeping up, Bishop Early looked at him strangely.

"You must come from good folks," he said. "You work hard and you got good ideas. What you wanna be?" he asked, settling back in his own barber chair, hands folded across his stomach. Roundhead didn't hesitate. "I wanna be a writer," he said, the passion welling in his throat. He looked away, afraid the Bishop might laugh. But he didn't.

"If you want it, that's what you'll be. Why you wanna be a writer?"

"Because I like to read good stories, and I think I can write 'em. Like, I can write better than those people at the *Call and*

Post!" said Roundhead, forgetting himself. "You see all the misspelled words in there?"

Bishop Early did laugh this time. "So, you can write better than them college-educated Negroes at the *Call and Post,* can you?" Roundhead looked down at his shoes and shook his head as if to apologize.

"Oh, I believe you, son. I ain't never had no use for them scandal sheets myself. Nothing in 'em except foolishness anyway." The Bishop paused, then said to Roundhead, wearily, "I just wanna tell you one thing, son."

"What?" Roundhead asked.

"Don't never let nobody take a razor to your head or neck like we do in here," he said. "Only poor people want razor lines. They cause you to break out, get ingrown hairs. Don't never forget that — OK?" Bishop Early said earnestly.

Roundhead nodded and left Bishop Early to close up the shop. Why had he told him about razor lines and what did it mean? It stayed with him even though he didn't understand.

The Contest

Columbian School began to separate the children according to academic ranking from the fourth grade on, and those who tested well and maintained their grades were put in the highest level of each grade. The average boys and girls ended up in the second level. Those who were below average in some way, informally known as the retards, were placed in the lowest level.

Children could be merciless in their indictments of each other on the basis of achievement, skin color, height, weight, speech differences, and, of course, gender. Any defect in a child's character made him fair game. While every school undoubtedly had its share of such competitiveness, Columbian, as an all-black school, represented the best and the worst of that tradition. Best in the sense that the children were pushed to improve academically through subtle but effective use of a growing racial awareness. Worst because a cloud of inferiority and desperation hung over the heads of these black children, who knew that the world they were about to enter viewed them as second class.

Roundhead sensed, because of the constant sorting, shifting, and relabeling of children as smart, dumb, stupid, gifted, and so on, that there was only room for so many of them at life's table. The administration confirmed that by preselecting, and in a sense predetermining the success of, only a handful of students as early as the fourth grade. Those who confirmed the administration's self-fulfilling prophecies were rewarded with special attention and encouragement, not to mention the best teachers in the school.

Selected from the beginning as bright but underachieving, Roundhead at first had more than a little trouble living up to everyone's expectations. He liked school because it took his mind off home. But it wasn't challenging enough to prompt him to obey the teachers without argument or questioning. Roundhead's favorite word — "Why?" — became a battle cry with his teachers, whose favorite answer — "Because I said so!" — seemed insulting and meaningless.

His sixth grade teacher, Mrs. Hudson, a highly dedicated black professional who took her role-modeling function seriously, told Roundhead he had to make an outline before he wrote his book reports. But outlines frustrated Roundhead. He liked to write and ramble as he did so, letting one idea lead to another. But Mrs. Hudson only knew one way to write a paper.

What changed her attitude was a writing contest.

"Class, the public library is having an essay contest, and Columbian School is going to put its best foot forward. The subject is 'What Books Mean to Me,' and I'm going to give you time to work on your paper today, in class. First, you'll do an outline—"

Roundhead sighed and put his head on his desk. Eventually he stopped listening, picked up a pencil, and began to write his essay. The topic delighted him. Books had saved his life in ways he never dreamed possible. He learned many lessons about life—that he wasn't the only child to suffer, that his travails could be overcome—from characters who seemed as alive to him as his own kinfolk. Bigger Thomas, Huck Finn, David Copperfield, Oliver Twist—these were the people he lived with, in a way, and their stories became his story.

Sparked by a passion to entertain and inform, Little Roundhead crafted a funny, highly detailed story about being kidnapped by Robert Louis Stevenson and taken for a ride down the Mississippi by Mark Twain. He put his whole heart into the telling of the story, hoping to make people feel as if they could touch the black waters of the Mississippi and taste his terror at being among pirates. At the end he said that books didn't mean quite as much to him as mashed potatoes, but they were still important. At the end of the day, he turned it in to Mrs. Hudson.

"What is this?" she asked, then read the top line: "What Books Mean to Me." "This is not an outline!"

"Miss Hudson, I told you, I don't like to do outlines

'cause it makes me say everything twice and I don't wanna say everything twice. I want to say it once!"

"You know the rules—you must do an outline. The problem with you, boy, is you're stubborn. You want to do everything your way!"

Roundhead picked up his books and walked out of the room without saying another word. He knew it would do no good to argue with her. She'd just have to read the essay to find out what he was talking about.

Days passed without any word about the contest or his essay. Finally, weeks after the other children had turned in their stories, Mrs. Hudson announced that the winners had been chosen. Roundhead's heart sank. He began to feel that he'd made a big mistake and would probably be disqualified for not writing an outline.

"We have two winners from Columbian elementary," she said, and with great ceremony she called Little Roundhead's name along with Diane Denora's. Roundhead wasn't the only one shocked by this turn of events. His classmates stared at him as if they couldn't believe their ears. Little Roundhead—the class clown and misfit—had won something for the first time in his life. The children looked at him blankly and stirred uneasily in their desks, and suddenly Roundhead began to feel as though he might faint. He didn't know what to do, so he covered his head with his hands, causing some of the children to laugh.

Soon he and Diane Denora were told to get ready to dress up in their Sunday best because they were going to the public library to read their essays before a group of teachers and librarians. On that day everything changed. Miss Coyle, his fifth grade teacher, hugged him, saying, "You see what happens when you do your best work? I'm so proud of you!"

Mrs. Hudson excused them for the afternoon, and they were given a private luncheon, away from the other children. Mr. Baldini came out of his office (a rare occurrence) to shake Roundhead's hand and tell him he had the makings of a fine boy, indeed. A boy who would grow up to make his parents proud.

Mother came to sit in the front row and listen as Roundhead got up in front of the librarians and teachers and read his essay. No fear intruded, no sense of worthlessness dogged the boy. He read from his heart, knowing that it was heart that silenced the room as he read. It was heart in the form of fantasy and deep love for words that took them all on his journey. He could see from the glow on their faces that they wanted to go, and all he had to do was give them the right words in the proper order and the whole audience would sail out of the room with him. And if they didn't love him when he started to read, they would fall in love with both the story and its creator by the time it was over.

As he listened to the other students from across the city read their essays, he came to believe that what Miss Coyle had said to him in fifth grade: he did have ideas and he knew how to express them in a way that inspired laughter and joy. The audience roared at his essay, and for the first time, he began to hear the faint sound of his own voice bursting through the words. By the time the audience applauded, he had taken the first step toward discovering not only what he wanted to do with his life but how he wanted to do it.

Love and War

In January 1963, Roundhead's last year of elementary school, he fell in love with a cute light-skinned girl name Patricia who lived two blocks away from his house on Goodman Street. Smitten with the kind of love only little boys are capable of, Roundhead decided to buy Patricia a present. He asked Mother for suggestions but came prepared with his own, to see if she would approve.

"It's nice to get a girl a present," Mother said warily, "but don't get carried away. You're only eleven. You're too young to be—"

"I'm not too young! She's the same age as me and she likes me."

"What'd she do, try to peck you on the cheek?" Mother teased.

"How about flowers?"

"Flowers? That's expensive!"

"I got the money."

Roundhead showed her his precious twenty-dollar bill. There was more where that came from, stashed in the cigar box beneath his bed. One reason he never cleaned under there was that he knew Mother and Father turned away in disgust each time they dared to look underneath it. At one time, Roundhead had more than a hundred dollars saved in that little El Producto box.

"You may have the money, but that's not the point. Flowers to a girl at your age—her mother might not like it. You ever think of that?"

He hadn't. This whole girl and gift thing was turning out to be more complicated than he had expected. He went to his room, closed the door, and thought about it—for five minutes. It was a toss-up between the beautiful red roses he had seen at the store on Burnet and Highland Avenues or a Bunn candy bar. The pros and cons sorted themselves out. He bought her the thing he liked better because he'd be able to defend himself against the charge of extravagance. This would be the first of many presents. Why not start small and build up—to, say, a nice Whitman's Sampler—after they'd confirmed the full import of this love?

Roundhead bought the Bunn bar and took it directly to Patricia's house after school. All day long he felt a mixture of warmth for and fear of the cute little girl with the pert nose and long limber legs. Patricia could do double Dutch rope jumping and play foursquare and still be every inch a lady-like little girl. He had watched her jump rope many a day, and although she'd never said more than "Hi" to him, Roundhead's intuition told him that she was deeply and hopelessly in love, just as he was.

Mustering all of his nerve, he bounded up to her front door and rang the bell. Mrs. Patricia—a big duck-faced woman with her daughter's potential for beauty that had, alas, remained unfulfilled—opened the door and stood staring down at him as if he were an orphan. Clutching the Bunn bar behind his back, Roundhead asked for Patricia, who apparently heard her name and came running to the door, where she slid under her mother's elbow and stood face to face with Roundhead. Sensing what was coming, Mrs. Patricia left immediately and the two lovers mooned at each other for all of three seconds before Roundhead blurted out, "Here's a present I bought for you," whereupon he thrust the Bunn bar at her. The little girl snatched the candy, laughed in Roundhead's face, and slammed the door. Roundhead tried to look at the bright side of things: at least she had taken the candy. They would talk and make plans like real lovers on the morrow. Clearly, Roundhead's view of love had been shaped by *The Donna Reed Show* and Loretta Young, not personal experience.

The next day at school, the children stared at Little Roundhead and laughed in derision as soon as he entered the playground. Those who laughed the hardest that morning were girls, some of whom he didn't even know. His buddy Francine sought him out immediately.

"What's this I hear about you giving Pat some cheap, melted candy?" she said in her usual blunt backwoods way.

"Who told you that?" Roundhead shouted.

"Everybody knows all about it. Pat told the whole school. You better find her, or it'll be on WCIN in a few minutes." WCIN, the local soul station, had everyone's ear in the Negro community. Francine was kidding, of course. Or was she?

"She said it was melted?" he asked in despair.

Roundhead frantically searched the school grounds for the cute little face of his betrayer. He found her sitting on the ground surrounded by a bunch of giggling, diffident girls. Roundhead stopped a minute and considered saying hello, but his boy genes kicked in, and he ended by walking away from the girls in total embarrassment.

He had been made a fool in love by being so trusting and by making assumptions about Patricia's feelings. It wouldn't be the last time. Francine caught him at lunch (which he ate with his head down in the cafeteria). "You know what?" she asked. "Pat already has a boyfriend."

"She does? Who?" Little Roundhead demanded.

"I don't know him. He goes to Ach Junior High and he's in eighth grade."

Roundhead felt a sinking feeling in his stomach. Patricia not only didn't love him, she was involved with one of those pinheaded bullies who went to the worst school in the city. Samuel Ach was known as the junior high for kids who wanted to become boxers, bouncers, or brassiere testers.

Every now and again, the school graduated someone who might go on to be a gym teacher, maybe even a coach. But this was the kind of school where the tardy bell served as the two-minute warning for the fight in the hall.

This news was all he needed to ruin an already crappy day. But he learned that you never can tell what strange things will happen when you suffer. Sometimes you can be rewarded, the way Roundhead was during science class. He drew Michelle Pritz for a lab partner and as they dissected a cow's eyeball, Michelle, the prettiest girl in the class, flirted with him by batting her long eyelashes and prancing around the Bunsen burner, flapping her skirt. Then she volunteered that she thought giving candy to Patricia was "awfully sweet and kind and lovely," and Roundhead thought he'd found his soulmate. A high-yellow girl from the East Coast who wore white cotton gloves to school every day in the fall and winter, Michelle made everyone feel inferior. Her parents had a little money, or so it was said, and she just knew she was better than all the rest of the children.

A few weeks later, Mrs. Hudson and Miss Coyle selected the children who would be the host and hostess of the variety show, an announcement the school awaited with great eagerness. When the news came over the loudspeakers, Roundhead nearly fell down the stairs as he heard his name and that of Michelle Pritz. What luck! Now they would be able to work together every day after school. Their romance appeared to be written in the stars. When Michelle found Roundhead outside the stage door, she threw her arms around him and gave him a big squeeze. "I knew you'd be the one," she said, grinning, and Roundhead looked at her with pathetic gratefulness and stifled his urge to sob. Life was just too good now that Michelle had shown her love for him.

"I just know we'll be great together," Little Roundhead sighed. On stage the two lovers projected the kind of chemistry that marked the great romances of the age: Fred and Ginger, Tracy and Hepburn—Dean Martin and Jerry Lewis.

Lindsay Brooks took offense at the many hours Roundhead and Michelle spent rehearsing. Lindsay had been courting Michelle for several years, but she had little interest in him because of his color. He wasn't just black, but a deep, purple kind of black, and Michelle didn't even seem colored to the rest of the children. She was what Mother called "too cute." She wore the best clothes, spoke in perfect English, got good grades, and wore her hair in Shirley Temple ringlets.

In those days, the courting process was called making time. A boy tried to hang out with a girl to see what kind of person she was. Sex was not an issue for Roundhead, who knew nothing about it and had been taught that such things were for married people. And since it led inevitably to kids, Roundhead didn't mind foregoing this mysterious pleasure. It was more than enough to be loved by someone as beautiful as Michelle and, in return, he would love her back— better than he loved anything except maybe reading. And baseball. And food. And writing . . .

Somehow Lindsay got wind of the fact that after one rehearsal Roundhead and Michelle were kissing backstage. Backstage kissing is a revered tradition of the theater, and usually means "Oh, God, I'm so scared of performing! I need your love to help me get through this!" At the time, the kissing seems important because it helps to reinforce the ensemble quality of a performance, but the epoxy is weak and may not even last as long as the cast party. The person who is kissed most passionately at the start of rehearsal will likely be hated before the end of the play. This is known as Barrymore's law.

But Roundhead was different. The kiss enchanted him, and he pined to start the cycle all over again: flowers and chocolates and walking her home—the whole shadow play. The disaster with Patricia had been a fluke. By contrast, Michelle was not only available but willing to take his arm after school in front of the other boys as they went off to rehearsal. Surely he couldn't be misreading these signs. And then there was that time she slipped and said, "I love you, too." This was memorable because the other two thousand times Roundhead had declared his undying affection had been met with timid smiles at best.

In this particular case, he hadn't misread the signs, but Lindsay Brooks had other ideas. Whenever he could, he trapped Michelle in a corner and started talking to her, touching her auburn curls, staring deeply into her light brown eyes. For about two weeks, Lindsay even came to rehearsals to keep an eye on Michelle until Miss Coyle tossed him out. But one day, Miss Coyle didn't arrive until later and the rambunctious children were left to their own devices. Michelle and Roundhead instantly took over and organized the rehearsal as they had seen Miss Coyle do. Roundhead took special joy in kicking Lindsay out, but he refused to leave.

"You don't belong here, man. Hit the road before I put you out myself," Roundhead said, rolling his shoulders like Humphrey Bogart did in the movies. He could hear the gangster music in his head as he stood his ground and stared a hole into Lindsay.

This turned out to be a serious mistake. Deadly silence gripped the auditorium as the two boys squared off. Although he was slightly smaller than Roundhead, Lindsay had a reputation as the kind of fighter who bit, kicked, and gouged his opponent—the kind of tactics rarely seen outside of cockfighting, and certainly not among honorable men.

"When you get done, we'll be waiting on you outside," Lindsay said and left.

Roundhead suffered through the whole rehearsal knowing that he would have to fight Lindsay before walking Michelle home. He asked the pert little beauty what she thought would happen. "I don't know," she said flippantly, "but I don't see why you two should be fighting over me."

They were fighting over her because she had played the two of them off against each other, and she knew it. Her answer stunned Little Roundhead and sent panic to every part of his body. Here he was ready to fight and die—well, at least bleed a little bit—for the most beautiful girl he'd ever met, and she acted as if she didn't care. It was a devastating, bitter moment.

After rehearsal, he took Michelle by the hand and led her outside onto the plaza, where a crowd of boys stood with their hands in their pockets, waiting for Roundhead. In their midst was Lindsay.

"I'ma kick your ass," he said and immediately charged Roundhead, who was still holding Michelle's hand when the attack occurred. He hit the ground hard with Lindsay on top of him, which could have been a good thing because Roundhead preferred wrestling to boxing. He scissored Lindsay with his powerful lower legs and struggled to turn him over. The combatants were surrounded by at least twelve other boys. Just as Roundhead landed a blow to Lindsay's chest and flipped him over, he felt a hard thumping kick to his head, followed by several more blows to his face and neck delivered by hobnailed boots. Roundhead covered up as best he could, but the damage had been done. He lay sprawled on the ground in a pool of blood from his nose and mouth as he saw the last of the boys scatter. Someone came back to check his pockets, and he passed out.

He awoke with Mr. Mann, the gym teacher, standing over him, ready to give him mouth-to-mouth resuscitation. The idea of mouth-to-mouth from Mr. Mann jarred the boy to full consciousness. "Don't move," said Mr. Mann. "Who did this?" he asked angrily.

"I don't know. Somebody stomped me," said Roundhead. He sat up looking for Michelle, but as he tried to focus he got woozy again. Mr. Mann put a handkerchief around his head. "I'll take you home," he said. Mr. Mann, one of the few white teachers at Columbian, had never before seemed particularly interested in anything but his own health. Famous for eating nothing but fruit at every lunch, Mr. Mann also taught sex education by showing a notorious film that every boy in sixth grade had been looking forward to seeing since kindergarten.

"We've got to put an end to this fighting. Who was it?"

"Lindsay Brooks," Roundhead answered.

"Huh—figures. That whole family's trouble," he said. "He's flunking on top of it. I've been teaching here a lot of years, and I've never seen . . ." Mr. Mann trailed off. "He's a new breed."

"Whatdya mean?" Roundhead's ears perked up.

"I mean he's been messing with girls in the hallway, skipping class. He's got no sense of decency—him and a couple of other boys. I'm going to report this to Baldini if it's OK with you."

Roundhead said wearily, "I don't mind." Mr. Mann gave him a puzzled look and then asked, "You all over that court stuff?"

Roundhead shook his head. "It's over but . . . it's not. People keep coming at me. I wish we could move."

Mr. Mann nodded. "They'd just find you. What you have to do is be smarter. Outsmart the bastards! You're a bright boy. You can think better and faster than they can."

When they arrived at home, Mother was standing out in front of the house with her arms crossed, looking up the street in the direction of the school. Her face turned ashen as she saw the car pull up and a white man disembark. She recognized Mr. Mann, who introduced himself. "Your son was in a fight at school. I don't know how badly hurt he is, but you might want to take him across the street to be checked."

Mother thanked him, brought her son inside, and began quizzing him like she was Allen Ludden on the *GE College Bowl*. When Roundhead told her that he and Lindsay had fought over Michelle Pritz, Mother gave him one of those stop-the-traffic looks she'd inherited from Grandmama.

"I told you not to get all involved in this mess with girls," said Mother. "It's not worth the trouble, believe you me."

At school the next day, Mr. Baldini conducted a complete investigation and called Lindsay's parents. He gave Lindsay a three-day suspension. The boys who'd kicked Roundhead were taken out of school and brought to Columbian to be identified. There, Roundhead heard the principal condemn the incident as hooliganism, and shortly after that a Cincinnati policeman from the juvenile division walked in, handcuffed the three culprits, and led them away, leaving Mr. Baldini to caution Roundhead about fighting.

"As many times as I've paddled you since kindergarten,

I should think you'd have gotten the message," Baldini said. Roundhead looked up at the principal and asked, through tears of frustration, "What am I gonna do? Run home every day? I gotta fight back."

Baldini leaned back in his wooden chair and put his feet up to consider the dilemma. He peered at Roundhead through one eye and chuckled. "Maybe you're just going to have to try harder to get along. Or pick different friends. Or use your head and outwit these guys."

Roundhead despaired of ever understanding girls and vowed to give them up—until they made more sense to him.

The second thing he did was think hard about how to make himself scarce among the other animals in the jungle: Operation Cheetah. He would do his best to outwit his opponents. But if it was not possible, he would have to hurt them. It was time to take better care of himself.

Soon afterward, Roundhead caught double pneumonia and was so sick he not only had to stay home from school but, to breathe at all, he had to sit in a hot tub and inhale the steam. The boy dragged his body, like a limp dishrag, from bed to bath and back again, trying to find some comfort. Finally Mother said, "We're going to see Dr. Katz," and she bundled her child in as many clothes as she could get on him and took him on the bus downtown.

Dr. Katz, his father, and his brothers were all physicians and great humanitarians who donated their medical expertise to poor families in nearly every part of the world. Richard, one of the brothers, had been Grandmama's family doctor since she had come to Cincinnati. He worked in an ancient medical facility that looked like a business office, with translucent glass panels and mahogany doors in the patient waiting rooms. It seemed that every time Roundhead visited, some child was screaming his lungs out behind one of those doors. The place smelled of alcohol and medicines Roundhead could only imagine the uses of.

Dr. Katz listened to Roundhead's lungs and said, "He's very sick. Might need to be hospitalized." Mother didn't want her boy in a hospital, even though she'd worked in them all of her life. She would do the nursing, thank you; the doctor's role was to pass the medicines. Dr. Katz gave Little Roundhead a shot of penicillin, and the boy never flinched. It was all he could do to catch a breath now and then that didn't have a death rattle at the core of it. He wanted desperately to sleep without the pain in his lungs. On the bus home, he finally achieved his goal—deep slumber—only to be awakened to get off the bus and walk home, supported by Mother.

Roundhead's sickness kept him at home for two whole weeks. He'd never been out of school for more than two days before. Mrs. Hudson called to see how he was doing. She sent homework, even, along with a jocular note intended to cheer Roundhead up. But he was too sick to care. Mother took him back to Dr. Katz several times, who gave him more penicillin. At the end of the first week, he felt better and went outside to play, thinking he'd been cured. But he caught a cold on top of the double pneumonia, and soon he was back in bed, under the covers, wondering what he had done to deserve all this misery.

His sickness forced him to lie in bed quietly, too tired to read but awake enough to think, to wonder, to dream. Viewing his future through the fog of fear and regret, Roundhead came to see that although many adults cared about his welfare, only he could take care of himself. As he lay there, he began to think about Father, whose attitude toward him had hardened since he'd been molested. He had wanted his son to fight back, understandably, in every possible way. That had been the nub of his criticism of Roundhead.

"You should have fought him, you should have killed him!" Father's words echoed through Roundhead's fevered brain. He had a dream like a cartoon in which he stood at the edge of the rec center and threw punch after punch until he could punch no more. Then an ambulance came to take him away. Once he was inside, the ambulance driver told him what was wrong: "You ain't supposed to be hitting everybody—just the guys wearing the red shirts." Then the driver stopped the ambulance and let Little Roundhead out at school, but no one was there. He spoke with the janitor, who told him that school was over for him and if he didn't leave soon, "Someone will come and put you back up in here. Now, you don't wanna go back up in here, do you?" Roundhead woke up sweating and murmuring. Mother fed him Campbell's chicken noodle soup, and gradually the little beanhead got better.

He could breathe again, eat solid food, and even read. Mother made him stay home two extra days to be sure he had recovered. When he was finally able to go back to school, Mrs. Hudson greeted him warmly, but she was obviously preoccupied. A big box of number two pencils sat on her desk along with a set of booklets. The class seemed unusually quiet, tense. Mrs. Hudson announced, "Class, today we are taking the Auburn Hills college preparatory test."

Some children laughed while others squirmed in their seats. But everyone—everyone—knew that this was a time for separating the average or even the clever kids from the very smartest of the bunch—a time of demarcation and departure into a future that, in a sense, had been predetermined. No class in the building took the test except the thirty-five students in the highest level of sixth grade. Only six would do well enough to be accepted. One of those six, a white boy named Emil Carson, a math genius, refused the opportunity, saying that the nearby district school was good enough for him. Another of the six had a borderline score and needed the permission of his principal in order to march into his future.

Little Roundhead's parents came to school to talk with Mr. Baldini. Should the boy be given a chance to study at the most prestigious school in the city? He didn't hear the conversation, but he was certain it went something like this:

"Your son has ability—he passed the test, but just barely. I'm concerned he may not be emotionally mature enough. He's underage as it is."

"I am certain he can handle it," Mother would have said. "He can do anything he puts his mind to."

"Now, baby, let the man say what he got to say. Go on, Mr. Baldini."

"Well, it's up to me. I can let him go. But it might do more harm than good, if he can't keep up with the others."

"I'm sure he'll be fine," Mother probably said, standing up abruptly.

And with that, Little Roundhead set off on the biggest adventure of his young life. He was on his way to Auburn Hills High School.

Coming into His Own

The Auburn

High on the hill, thy stately dome we see
symbol of honor, truth and loyalty,
Auburn Hills High, thy name we sing with pride
through out our lives for'er be our guide!
Sursum Ad Sunum — thy motto we uphold
We thrill to thy banner — Blue and Gold
So Rise to the Highest
our voices loudly cry —
we'll bring fame and glory
to Auburn Hills High!

Unique by virtue of its public status, the Auburn was a college prep institution for grades seven through twelve with a tradition of academic excellence virtually unparalleled in the nation. Many well-known individuals — including the 1920s sex vamp Theda Bara, Yippie leader Jerry Rubin, and hundreds of the best lawyers and doctors in the world — had graduated from the school since it opened in 1895. The educational hopes and dreams of many a parent centered on their children's admission to Auburn Hills.

Trouble was, admission was selective. Students in elementary schools across the city were told in sixth grade, weeks in advance, that they would be taking the "Auburn Hills test."

The students would report this bit of news to their parents, who invariably panicked. Admission to Auburn Hills was considered the key to future achievement not only in college but in the rest of life. The reason was simple: Auburn Hills High School put unrelenting pressure on every student to fulfill his or her potential.

Roundhead had never even seen the school. His family had no car, and nothing in his life had prompted him to walk the five miles out of his neighborhood into totally unknown territory. Born with little sense of direction, Roundhead had no idea that if he had continued walking down School Street, where Columbian School reposed in its gothic splendor, down the Rockdale Hill, he would have come to a beautifully forested part of his city, where signs of a slightly more prosperous life lived by other Negroes might have stunned him. For in the valley below were acres of greenery so lush they seemed to have been painted by the hand of God. Had he crossed the huge street called Victory Parkway and wandered through the woods, he would have discovered steps built into the hillside where other pilgrims had marched before him in search of wisdom. Partially hidden by the foliage was the Auburn itself, modeled on Thomas Jefferson's Monticello, with a huge rounded dome, pillars, and a granite stairway intended to intimidate.

In the summer after sixth grade, Roundhead and other "at risk" students attended remedial classes at the Auburn. He read at the tenth grade level, but math was a different story. His brain literally seemed to go blank when he stared at numbers. During summer school, the "at risk" newcomers like Roundhead had a chance to experience the school in a nonpressured environment. Roundhead soon discovered that he had never been inside a building more dedicated to learning, more serious about character, more steeped in tradition. The Auburn had Greek statues in the hallways, bright fluorescent lighting everywhere, and a solid tradition concerning the classroom demeanor of its students. That summer, Roundhead made friends with other seventh graders who were in the same position he was—flattered to be there but scared to death of failure.

Before classes began in the fall, the school called an assembly of all seventh graders and their parents. There, in the massive auditorium, Roundhead and hundreds of others listened nervously to the principal of AHHS, who stood before them in a crew cut and a dark blue suit.

"You, children, are the leaders of tomorrow! Auburn Hills High School demands achievements of the highest order and will accept no less. Parents, make note of this—your child will have one hour of homework for each course every night!"

A collective gasp went up from the auditorium. "That means, if you want to play sports, you'll be awfully tired in the mornings. Because while we value athletics here, we place the emphasis on academics."

The principal told the truth. In Roundhead's first year at AHHS, his shortcomings were highlighted by every teacher he had. He took Latin I and flunked it for the year. He took Math I and flunked that, too. The only reason he didn't get kicked out was that he had two A's—one in English, the other in music. Anything less than a C average resulted in immediate dismissal after the second report period. Roundhead came out of his last class one day to find a line of weeping boys and girls winding its way to the counselor's office: they were trying to beg their way back into the school. Their report cards had come out with an asterisk at the top, the symbol of failure at the Auburn. More than one student over the years had committed suicide because he hadn't measured up.

Roundhead had no choice but to work hard. He had no desire to go backward, and besides, there were so many things to learn. He discovered the joy of diagramming sentences, a skill that seemed silly at first but later came to be an important editorial tool. He learned that singing, which he could do very well, was an art, not just a gift, and that free expression of it was good for his spirit. No one had ever told him that before, and the affirmation made an important difference in the quality of his life.

Roundhead made friends, genuine companions, for the first time in his life during seventh grade. These were children like him—social outcasts who loved learning but didn't fit in. Friends like Homer, a light-skinned black student with red hair and freckles who invented the Pyro Maniacs, an informal group of kids who lived to set small, controlled fires; Bernard Isserwitz, a short, affable Jewish kid who later founded the Model Rocket Club; Donald Lipsky, known as Rabbi to his friends, a big-hearted extrovert who embraced life and everyone in it; Sarah Tunney, a beautiful brown-haired WASP girl who turned into a cold-hearted, class-conscious snob; Arlana Brewster, easily the most popular and beautiful girl in the class; Sharon Darwin, a brilliant black girl who overcame her lack of physical beauty to become a popular leader and a great academic talent; Heinz Grunsteen, the astute cold-blond boy who caught hell from some of the Jewish kids because of his German background; Alonzo Breeson, a short, light-skinned middle-class black kid who dressed meticulously and had only two interests— girls and sex; and Ronnie Toliver, a "greaser" wannabe who tinkered with cars and eventually married his childhood sweetheart. These were Little Roundhead's first friends at the Auburn, and they supported him simply because they liked him, something he had rarely found in his own community.

Roundhead discovered that he was more popular with girls than he thought he would be, mostly because he had been hurt in love and wanted nothing more than friendship from them. His best friend for many years, Sue Ann Grabowski, a buxom, bubbly girl from the suburbs with more energy and personality than any one person had the right to have, was generous with her time and love. She sought out Roundhead for reassurance and friendship. He needed her warmth and her sense of humor.

Roundhead liked girls, especially Sue Ann, but the idea of sex had been tainted by his experience of abuse. In those days, sexual activity before adulthood in most circles was considered a sure sign of bad character. Girls wore girdles and garters and as much makeup as they could get away with, and some tried to "walk the walk" of precocious sexuality, but only a minority of students went "all the way," and they were marked as reckless individuals. Roundhead's generation would later make sexual activity a sort of national pastime, along with smoking dope, dropping acid, and questioning authority. But in the early fall of 1963, other issues occupied their minds.

Imagine a group of children fresh out of grade school scrambling to find their classes, all of them holding a dozen books in their little arms. That's what the hallways looked like during the first week of school at Auburn Hills. Seventh graders, called Effies because many of them were destined to flunk out during the first year, cluttered the halls in search of their classrooms. Dire predictions—like "one-third of you will not be here for graduation" —came from the teachers during the first weeks of school. The sheer stress of knowing that anyone could fail at any moment, regardless of skin color, family, money, or origin, motivated most students to study hard and to do what they were told. The option to question the teacher's authority was always open. In fact, questioning became another way to test the truth, and Roundhead found himself in a kind of Socratic heaven where he was free to prove the teacher wrong, if he could.

This atmosphere of academic freedom led to a few wild acts among students —like the founding of the Joe Wheel Club, which sought to discover precisely how far a pumpkin thrown from a moving car could roll —but from the beginning, students were taught to take responsibility for their actions. Teachers carefully and sympathetically sought out those who clearly hadn't been prepared for a school where the light of academia shone so brightly and worked with students one on one. Among Roundhead's favorite classes was one on Sino-Soviet totalitarianism, in which the myth of communism as savior was dissected with wit and zeal by Professor Henrietta Von Russo; Other favorite subjects were American history, taught by Anthony Whittaker, who burned his draft card in front of Roundhead's class and encouraged civil disobedience; English lit, taught by at least three different professors who had varied but equally exciting approaches; and geometry, presided over by Professor Illyavich, a bald middle-aged man who often lectured while standing atop his desk.

With this kind of eccentricity among the teachers, the students felt encouraged to experiment with everything from clothing to makeup to drugs to gender transformation. Finally, Roundhead had discovered a place where his style and sensibilities seemed absolutely middle-of-the-road, inoffensive, acceptable to most if not all.

During that hectic first year, however, Roundhead learned that the school actually encouraged cliques rather than individualism. Students tended to gang up—the jocks, the greasers, the hippies, the WASPS, the snobs—but each group tended to be on the lunatic fringe of the main stream. The few students from Columbian, all black, never gave each other the time of day after arriving at the Auburn. Auburn Hills became their first opportunity to be part of the mainstream rather just another group of colored youngsters struggling for recognition. This new opportunity made social interaction a veritable laboratory of multiculturalism. But the crushing weight of all that homework deterred an active social life. At the Auburn, seventh grade was about learning to tread water.

Shortly after he began his first year at the Auburn, as Roundhead was about to get off the bus to come home, he saw a group of rowdy boys from his neighborhood standing on the street corner. He knew instantly that they were waiting for him. As he stepped off the bus, the boys pushed him down, took his book bag, and threw his Latin book into the sewer. Their chief complaint—that Roundhead considered himself better than them because he went to the Auburn—both puzzled and frightened him. Immersed in his new school and new friends, Roundhead had forgotten the challenges that perpetually awaited him when he returned to his neighborhood.

A few days later, the same boys stood at the bus stop, but this time Roundhead had learned his lesson. He got off the bus at the stop before Goodman Street, cut through the old

General Hospital receiving ward, and crossed the street half a block from his home. He began to practice variations of this avoidance method, taking great enjoyment in beating his enemies in this game of wits. What Miss Coyle and Mr. Baldini had told him was true: he had infinitely more power over his fate than he had dared to imagine.

Writing

The *Chatterbox*, Auburn Hills' flagship student publication, prided itself on a kind of snappy, zippy student lingo that, while literate, took great pains to embrace the burgeoning youth culture of the 1960s. Almost immediately after school began, Roundhead forced himself to go to the first meeting of the *Chatterbox* staff, even though he was convinced he'd never have the chance to write. He had an interest in features, human stories about people. He was dismayed when one of the staffers said, "You look like you could do sports," and pointed him toward the next room. He didn't want to "do" sports, but soon he found himself trapped in the middle of a bunch of white guys in penny loafers who droned on and on about what kind of sports page they should have. Roundhead grew restless until the sports editor, Marvin Dimmler, posed this question: "Anybody free to go to Portsmouth Saturday night and cover our football game there?" In the room were six upper classmen, all of whom had seniority over Roundhead. But no one volunteered. He couldn't believe it. No one wanted to cover the first football game of the year? Instantly, he threw his hand in the air and waved it wildly. Amused by Roundhead's enthusiasm, Dimmler looked him up and down a minute and then said, "It's yours, sonny boy. You ride out with the team on the bus."

Roundhead could barely contain himself as he told Mother the good news. Her response? "Where's Portsmouth?" Roundhead didn't know, didn't care, and wanted only to celebrate his victory. He'd been given a chance to do what he'd always dreamed of—writing for publication.

His elation came crashing down when Father said, "You ain't going to no Portsmouth, boy. That's all there is to it."

"But you don't understand. They said I could—"

"I said you are not going!" Father yelled. "Now I don't want to discuss it."

All the weight of animosity Roundhead bore toward Father came rushing back to him. He had never argued with Father, fearing immediate punishment far out of proportion to what he deserved. But out of the hole in his heart, opened by his father, came these words:

"If you don't let me do this, I swear, I'll never speak to you again as long as I live!"

Father turned and stared at Roundhead in amazement. The boy went up to his room, closed the door, and tried to steady his nerves. He saw the dent he once put into the wall after he'd watched Father and Mother fight. He saw the plastic Father had put on the windows to keep the cold wind from chilling him at night. He knew that Father loved him in ways that seemed dutiful, not affectionate. But what kind of father would want to limit his son's opportunity?

What had happened to the Old Man when he was young that made him so unfeeling? The middle child in a family of seven that started out near Little Rock, Arkansas, and ended up moving to Chicago, Father had been babied by his mother, punished by his daddy. He seldom spoke of his childhood. It was as if he'd been born with his work clothes on. His daddy, Samuel, was older than his mother, Virginia, and tended toward harshness with the children, especially the boys. In fact, the oldest boy ran away from home at the age of fourteen to live with his aunt in St. Louis, swearing never to have anything to do with his daddy again.

Father was very young when the family moved to Chicago. They moved quickly, almost overnight, because something mysterious had happened in Little Rock—something involving a murder or a beating that one of the brothers had been involved in. That incident, pivotal to the family's history, remained a secret. When they were asked, relatives claimed they couldn't remember the details. But the family renamed itself in order to remain anonymous should anyone ask questions.

The options for black men growing up in the 1930s and 1940s were few. You could become a Pullman car porter or a postal worker or a preacher, if you were so inclined. Or you could join the army. Father had been told by someone, probably his daddy, that the military would teach him discipline. He was a playful kid with little knowledge of the world who had been taunted and teased by his older brothers. So he enlisted at the age of seventeen.

According to Father, the army made him one of the youngest buck sergeants in its history, and he found his niche as a molder of men. He never actually fought in a war, but he trained thousands of troops who were eventually sent to Korea. Later, he often expressed a profound dislike for the military.

While he was stationed at Fort Dix, New Jersey, he met his wife, one of the base accountants, who took a shine to the six-foot, 160 pound sergeant. As for courtship and the intimacies of new love, the children never heard any stories that suggested such things. They imagined Father and Mother meeting, looking each other in the eye, and jumping the broom as if they had no choice.

After the army experience, Father tried numerous ways to break into the job market, each unsuccessful. He went to radio and TV repair school, sold Avon, tried odd jobs. Eventually, he took the only job that would guarantee a steady income for his family—as a janitor. While he searched for the right occupation, he made weekly rounds to various merchants; he became the most articulate black man in the community. He treated the grocer, the hardware store owner, the pharmacist with great respect and perfect manners. And his sense of humor dazzled everyone. He knew exactly what to say to put a person at ease, and as a result he was very popular with people who were virtually strangers.

With his family, however, his demeanor was altogether different. There were times when Father lost patience with life itself and seemed hemmed in by his lack of opportunity. He had creative ideas, especially about household organization, and he was as responsible for cleaning and cooking as Mother in the early days of Roundhead's youth. But he never had the chance to use his brains for profit.

That evening, Roundhead lay on his bed, thinking about these things, trying to put a picture of his father's life together, when Mother knocked on the door. She sat on the edge of his bed and gazed at him fondly.

"You know that you are my heart," she said. "I love all my children, but with you it's always been special. So I want to tell you something. You may not realize it, but your father always wanted to be a writer."

Roundhead sat up, not believing his ears. "He did?"

"He's too proud to tell you that himself, and I don't want you to say anything about it to him," Mother said. "He never had the chances that you have, and I think that upsets him at times."

"But what about all the times he told me that writing was a waste of time, that I should learn to work with my hands?"

"He didn't mean it. You think about it, and we'll talk about it later," she said.

"I just have to go to Portsmouth to cover that football game. I can't believe they would even let me, but now that they have—"

"Don't worry about that," Mother said. "Good things happen to those who wait." She smiled and walked out of the room.

Roundhead wanted to ask Father why he wasn't able to articulate and achieve his dreams. He wanted to run to him and say, "Let's struggle together to be writers. You tell me your stories and I'll find the right words to express them." But instead, he kept his promise not to speak to the Old Man. For three days Roundhead simply looked away whenever he spoke, which normally would have resulted in his being slapped. This time, nothing happened.

Roundhead had made plans to leave the house on Saturday and take the bus to school in time to join the team. He realized that after the game was over they would be returning late, so he resolved to swallow his pride and ask one of the players for a ride home. He was going to cover the game, regardless of what Father said.

On Friday evening, Father relented for reasons that were unclear, although he remained sour about it, telling Roundhead again that "this writing stuff" was never going to lead to anything good. But Roundhead was so relieved by the fact that he had permission to go that he actually listened to Father this time and took it all in. "It" was a mishmash of criticisms about Roundhead not doing all his chores, about thinking that he was a man now, about being at Auburn Hills. Father's real complaint—that Roundhead had begun to develop his own strong personality and identity outside his father's sphere of influence—never surfaced.

But as Roundhead listened to the ranting and raving this time, he heard Father's concern that his son, a Negro, would set his hopes too high and end up frustrated, perhaps as he had. The world wasn't a fair place, and even if you had talent, you couldn't count on being accepted. What Father didn't understand was that the world was changing, gradually, and that his son would have opportunities he'd never dreamed of.

Oswald

On Friday afternoon, November 22, 1963, at about 2:00 eastern standard time, Little Roundhead had just completed his first pair of ill-made stilts in his least favorite class, shop. The principal's voice came over the loudspeaker, crackling with tension and, it seemed to Roundhead, something like dread. Apparently, events involving the president of the United States that day had gone terribly awry in Dallas, Texas. As the principal's voice gave way to a hysterical-sounding CBS radio news bulletin, the thirty or so boys began to inhale. By the time Douglas Edwards had finished, there was no more air left in the room.

The shop teacher, eccentric even in the best of times, stood before the astonished class and buried his head in his gnarled hands, sobbing. "You are all . . . excused," he murmured, but the boys could not move a muscle as they watched the white-haired teacher pull a handkerchief from his back pocket and wipe his rummy eyes.

Roundhead felt a shiver pass through the room as the collective fear and confusion fulminated. The boys turned to one another for silent consolation, thunderstruck by the implications of the bulletin. Amidst what can only be called group rigor mortis, Byron Green, a pale, epileptic child from a well-known Republican family uttered a single memorable sentence:

"Good! Now Nixon can get in!"

Later, on the hill outside the normally sedate prep school, a gaggle of boys more accustomed to playing tennis and golf than to engaging in fisticuffs jumped Byron Green and beat him as if they were beating a rug: routinely and in grim-faced silence. But Roundhead, in a daze after the news, could barely concentrate enough to board the right bus and get home. When he arrived, Mother was not watching *General Hospital* on ABC as usual but had switched to CBS and Walter Cronkite, who looked for all the world like a lost child.

It was then that Mother said something the boy would never forget: "Lord, I hope it wasn't a colored man." Little Roundhead tried to suppress the raw feelings bursting in his chest like a tidal wave of trepidation. He knew that Mother had been speaking for the whole colored world. Had the president been shot by a Negro, the black race never could have lived it down, that's all, and every black family in America would have been forced to begin their second great diaspora, this time to escape a volcano of hatred.

But very soon, the name Lee Harvey Oswald was on every tongue, and the worry shifted from protection of the race to protection of the nation. At the barbershop where Little Roundhead swept up on Saturday mornings, the main proprietor, Bishop Early, pronounced the murder a conspiracy.

"This much I know," said the rotund Bishop, wagging his finger in a patron's face, "ain't nobody can kill the president by theyself. They got to have help from the inside."

"Lyndon Johnson done it," said another man. "Wasn't nary a hair on his head touched—and in his own backyard, too."

"This man Oswald been in and out of Russia three, four times, that's all you need to know about this killing," a drunken patron in the barber's chair stammered. "Hey, hey, hey, Bishop! Ease up on that razor!"

"My fault—no blood drawn," said the bishop. "Now, the way I figure it, Secret Service pulled the trigger one way or another."

"What reason the Secret Service got to kill the president?" someone asked.

Another added, "The Secret Service is secret, Early! That mean you don't know a damn thing about it!"

The crafty bishop of the African Methodist Episcopal Church, a gentle, serious man who made his living as a barber during the week and thus studied the faces and the spirits of men from every angle, exhaled in frustration. The bishop had hired Roundhead a year ago and some months later patted him on the back and said, "I'ma give you a piece of advice, son, even though you didn't ask me for it: slow down and live a little. You work entirely too hard for being just eleven years old."

Now he walked to the middle of the cramped barber-shop, razor in hand, pushed his glasses back up the bridge of his pinched nostrils, and tilted his head slightly toward the heavens. This was his preaching posture, and once he assumed the position there was no stopping him.

"No matter who done it, there can be no reason for it as such," said Bishop Early, who knew how to talk proper when he wanted to. "Whosoever hath slain this president is accursed of God, like Judas Iscariot before him. Because Kennedy was a mighty good man," the bishop paused for dramatic effect, "even if he was Catholic!"

The next day, Sunday, November 24, Little Roundhead awoke to see the sun burning through the frost on his window. He rejoiced in its momentary warmth and rose quickly. He felt a smile coming on—this morning, he would be able to read the newspaper before anyone else.

Little Roundhead devoured the gritty details feverishly, trembling like a mouse in an earthquake—afraid of something but not big enough or smart enough to know what. A small paragraph in a wire-service story noted that "after the shots had been fired, Dallas police pulled their guns and charged up the hillside in the direction from which they thought the shots had come. They chased and apprehended a Negro man who had been running away with his daughter in his arms."

Roundhead sadly shook his head. As always, the first suspect had been a Negro man. The newspaper didn't say whether the Dallas police beat the poor soul, but Roundhead pictured him cowering and cradling his daughter, pleading for his life, and the image made him sick with rage and sorrow. These same feelings chilled him each time the white nurses from the nearby hospital decided to cross the street when they saw him, a black boy, coming toward them. He felt helpless, wounded, hurt by their presumptions about him and every other black male. And because Little Roundhead felt so many things so strongly so often, his heart had been deeply wounded by the age of eight, and his spirit carried a burden that had already deformed his childhood.

Roundhead reassembled the newspaper and flipped on

the television, looking for escape—*Bowery Boys, Little Rascals, Heckle and Jeckle*. Today, he needed their tomfoolery more than any tonic. But instead he saw jerky films of the president's motorcade speeding to Parkland Hospital in Dallas, of Lyndon Johnson being sworn in as president by a woman, of the grief-stricken first lady with her children, the Texas Book Depository, the grassy knoll. He heard eyewitnesses reciting the same confusing litany of facts: the shots that seemed to come from two places—above and below—the baffling murder of officer J. D. Tippett, and the apprehension of a man in a Fort Worth movie theater.

The facts were so confusing that at first Little Roundhead did not believe his own eyes or ears. This was like a nightmare made for TV. He moved closer to the set and turned up the sound. Someone said, "He has maintained his innocence from the beginning," and then the screen filled with reporters and people who appeared to be policemen from another planet—wearing Stetsons and stingy-brimmed hats, smoking hand-rolled cigarettes and speaking with the harshest kind of cracker accents. They all stood around looking comically incompetent, waiting, it seemed, for something to happen.

Baffled by what he saw and heard, Roundhead cranked the sound up yet again. "AND NOW, THEY ARE BRINGING LEE HARVEY OSWALD—" the reporter boomed.

"Turn that TV down! It's too early on a Sunday morning for all that noise!" Mother yelled.

Alert to something peculiar in the way the camera was positioned, Little Roundhead placed his face less than a foot away from the TV in order to get a closer look at this Oswald character. The camera bounced along behind the accused man, who was handcuffed and pinned between two bull-like policemen. Roundhead sat up suddenly, his eyes roaming the picture tube, taking in the mass of confusing messages.

"Oswald is being led past dozens of police detectives who are on the scene to ensure the security of—" the reporter was saying when from the lower right-hand corner of the screen a black blur darted into Oswald's path and made a barking noise.

"HE'S BEEN SHOT! OSWALD'S BEEN SHOT!" the reporter screamed. The camera went wild and Roundhead jumped up in the middle of the living room, tearing his hair out of his head, incredulous. "They shot him, Mama!" he yelled. "They shot him! Come quick!"

"Who shot who?" came the casual retort from Mother in the kitchen. Little Roundhead didn't know it then, but in the years that followed, that question would echo ceaselessly into his days and nights, haunting him, driving him to Dallas as a middle-aged man, where he would rent a room overlooking Dealey Plaza during the twentieth-anniversary reenactment of the assassination.

But on that particular Sunday in Dallas when Oswald was murdered in the custody of countless Dallas policemen and FBI agents, there was at least one black child in America who vowed never to be taken in by the grotesqueries of politics again.

Harmony

The sad closing days of 1963, when Roundhead and his generation lost a man who seemed utterly invincible, gave way in February 1964 to a weird kind of hysteria known as Beatlemania. Typical of the Auburn, discussions about the meaning of mass hysteria were sparked by the Fab Four.

Students at the Auburn were trained to talk a subject to death, to chew it up, spit it out, and reexamine it. Most of the boys thought the fuss about the Beatles was a little much and that men who wore long hair were queer.

Never was there a more perfect melding of inside and outside worlds than during this period, when the struggle for civil rights was embraced wholeheartedly by AHHS students and the idea of fighting for freedom took hold everywhere. Finally, AHHS and the rest of the world were somewhat in alignment.

Of course, this ferment wasn't going on in Roundhead's house. To escape Father's growing harshness, Roundhead busied himself with study and entrepreneurial activities. He still had three jobs on the weekend that kept him out of the house all day Saturday. At night, he would study in his room until he fell asleep.

Gradually, Roundhead noticed that both his parents were studying, too. After dinner, Father took out a heavy black book and a slide rule and began reading and calculating. He fell into the same kind of trance that overcame Roundhead and often worked long into the night. Mother also began to study at the dining room table, poring over nursing and pharmacology books. Both were as serious as he'd ever seen them. Roundhead asked Father what he was doing and why. Father's answer nearly knocked Roundhead over.

"I'm learning to be a fireman," he said.

"A fireman? What for?"

"Not that kind of fireman," he said. "I'm learning to operate boilers so I can become a steam fireman and advance myself." Then he went back to work.

Mother, too, explained that she wanted a better job and that education was the answer. As a licensed practical nurse she couldn't pass medicines without the approval of a nursing supervisor. She was determined to learn pharmacology so that her job at Shriner's Hospital would offer more authority and better pay.

"I'm learning to be a burn specialist," she said, and it was back to the dining room table for her.

Sometimes, when Roundhead had to prepare for a Latin test or write a paper for English lit, he felt lonely upstairs in his own room, so he would slip quietly into the dining room where Mother and Father were studying. He'd slide into a chair and open one of his books and begin studying. For the first time he felt that he and his parents were in harmony, working toward the same thing—the betterment of their family. He didn't know how to express it, but the house he'd lived in for so many years finally felt more like a home.

The *Call and Post*

From his days of climbing the General Hospital retaining wall to doing his first sports story, Little Roundhead had always sought personal fulfillment of an important dream. That dream took root when he won the Columbian School essay contest and developed even further through his work with the *Chatterbox*.

Something big pushed at Roundhead by the time he was fourteen and in ninth grade. He felt he hadn't done enough. His businesses were fine, although eventually Father made him quit going to Bishop Early's shop because he said he didn't like the company the Bishop kept. Faced with a drop in revenue, he had to come up with some other way to continue the progress he had made.

One cold day, after selling the *Call and Post* newspaper,

Roundhead the businessman took time out for lunch at the Red Barn hamburger shack. Red Barn burgers cost only fifteen cents, and that day he had earned a total of six dollars. His route had taken him far outside his own neighborhood into the territory of other foot soldier-salesmen. They would nod at each other knowing that it was a tough business, this selling of newspapers, because colored people didn't have the resources to buy the local black paper every week.

That Saturday, Roundhead read the newspaper he'd been selling. Seldom had he bothered to do this, since the stories were often poorly constructed and frequently inaccurate. But that afternoon, he read the entire newspaper from cover to cover. When he finished, he knew what he had to do.

With increasing excitement, he ran home and gathered up his articles from the *Chatterbox*, put them in a folder, and said to his mother, who was cooking chili and corn bread, "You know something, mama? I really *can* write better than those people who at the *Call and Post.*"

"I'm sure you can, honey," she said indulgently.

"I'm gonna go tell the man that!" Roundhead said.

"What man? Where you going so fast?"

"Mr. Baldwin. He's the editor. I'm gonna tell him, show him, I can write."

Roundhead bolted down the stairs and up the street to catch a bus to the newspaper office. During the ride, he shut out nervousness and negativity. He'd been selling the paper for years; it was time he met the editor. But what if he didn't like what Roundhead said about his newspaper? He wondered if his opinion would ruin the whole thing, make it appear that he was arrogant and boastful. He would simply have to find an acceptable way to say what he wanted to say.

The bus let Roundhead off one block from the *Call and*

Post office. The headquarters was in Cleveland but the Cincinnati office produced a few of the twenty or more pages. Roundhead came to the door and stopped. He had lost some of his nerve. What if the newspaper man laughed in his face? Worse still, what if he fired him?

Roundhead steeled himself as he opened the door. The place was dark because some of the burned-out fluorescent lights hadn't been replaced. Roundhead peered into the back office, where a slender black man wearing a white shirt and tie sat with his feet up on his desk. As he read the copy in his hands, he wore an expression of fatigue that is unique to editors: a mixture of eyestrain, disappointment, and disbelief.

Roundhead stood frozen in place at the front of the room, wondering what to do next. He shifted the folder he carried behind his back, suddenly hyperaware that he was just a kid and this, for all its faults, was a professional newsroom. He asked in a scratchy voice, "Uh, are you Mr. Baldwin? Alan Baldwin?"

The man slowly turned and looked at him.

"I need to talk to you, sir," Roundhead said softly, "about something important." The man didn't take his feet down from the desk. He dropped the manuscript he'd been reading and turned his head toward Roundhead.

"What?" he asked. "Somebody beat you up and take your papers or something?" He was only half joking.

"No, sir." Roundhead saw that Mr. Baldwin regarded him seriously, so he removed his cap and said, "Mr. Baldwin, no offense, sir, but I do believe I can write better than your reporters."

Baldwin said nothing, but his lip curled and he let out a slight chuckle. "Really?" he said finally. "What makes you think that?"

"Because, Mr. Baldwin, I have been selling this paper and reading it for five years."

Baldwin leaned back in his chair to regard the young man from a different perspective. "What's that you got—samples? Put them over here. I'll look at them later."

Something made Roundhead push again. "They're sports stories. I write for the newspaper at Auburn Hills High."

Baldwin sat up and took his feet off his desk.

"Really? Let me see them."

Roundhead handed him the folder and swallowed hard. Baldwin scanned the lead paragraph from the Portsmouth football game. "Good lead," he said, nodding.

Roundhead, numb with expectation, couldn't say anything. As Baldwin read the stories, he kept eyeing Roundhead, trying to get a fix on him. Roundhead looked down and away. When he looked up again, Mr. Baldwin was still reading.

Roundhead stood there for ten minutes, shaking with fear. He had the urge to bolt not once but twice. What kept him rooted there was a belief that if all else failed, he could start over again. If this man rejected his work or didn't like the cut of his coat, he comforted himself with the knowledge that once, not many years before, he had felt so bad that he almost killed himself. Nothing could ever be that bad again.

Baldwin put the package down, pursed his lips as he watched Roundhead shifting his weight nervously, then removed his feet from the desk. He opened the drawer and pulled out a white card on which he scrawled his name.

"Take this. The University of Cincinnati basketball team is playing the Louisville Cardinals next Saturday afternoon at the fieldhouse. I want you to write me a story about it. This will get you in free. Have the story on my desk Monday afternoon." Roundhead put his cap back on, took the card from

Baldwin's desk, and turned to leave. "I'm not saying I'll use it," Baldwin called out.

That Saturday, Roundhead left in the morning as usual on his paper route. Without telling Father, Mother, or anyone else, he cut short the route and walked to the University of Cincinnati fieldhouse. The attendants peered at Roundhead and his pass suspiciously before sending him to the press entrance. He arrived more than an hour before the game began because he was nervous and wanted to check out the entire stadium. Although he literally lived no more than fifteen minutes from the place they called the Cardiac Castle—because the university had won and lost a few heartbreakers there at the last minute—he'd never been on the university campus.

He watched the cheerleaders practice before the game and marveled at how much fun they were having. "So this is college," he thought to himself while he munched a hot dog with extra pickle relish. He studied both teams as they warmed up, looking hard for pregame indicators. These things he did out of sheer instinct, but in truth he could barely catch his breath. He was covering a University of Cincinnati basketball game as a reporter for a real newspaper. The feeling of freedom that came over him was an entirely new experience.

Just before the game started, he made his way to the press box, where he sat among a group of whiskey-drinking, cigar-smoking newspaper reporters, all white, all crude, all having a great time. They were pros, these guys, and most carried small portable typewriters that they punched with two fingers. Only Roundhead and a couple of college reporters used notebooks and pens.

The game ended with a spectacular flourish of baskets by both teams, who were battling for the lead in the old Missouri Valley Conference. With two seconds left, the Bearcats threw the ball to half court and one of their star players launched a satellite into orbit with no time remaining on the clock. The ball came down—swish—nothing but net. The University of Cincinnati had won at the last second, and the Cardiac Castle mystique continued.

Roundhead couldn't wait to get home to begin writing. He started his story in the press box and was so animated by what he had seen he could barely compose himself. What a game—what a life! To have so much freedom, to work using your brains as well as your senses! As he left the stadium and blended in with the last of the crowd, he felt calm and self-assured. He was going to be able to make a good story better by telling it well. That was all he had ever wanted to do.

Writing the story and rewriting it at least three times preoccupied Roundhead for the rest of the weekend. On Monday, he stopped at the *Call and Post* office hoping to see Mr. Baldwin personally, but the woman at the front desk said he was out. Roundhead left the story with her, asking her to please be certain that Mr. Baldwin saw it right away. When he tried to communicate urgency, Roundhead's voice went up an octave, which seemed to amuse the young woman.

Waiting—the worst thing in the world—became Roundhead's task. He drifted through his schoolwork Monday afternoon. Tuesday, he had no room in his head for anything but hope that Mr. Baldwin would like the story. So many deeply felt emotions rose up in Roundhead, so much yearning for something he had no right to expect, that he found himself drained and drifting into sleep in the last class of the day. By Wednesday, he had given up hope. Obviously, Mr. Baldwin would have called had he liked the article. Roundhead felt sluggish, disappointed, betrayed by his own dream. He rewrote the story many times in his head and decided that any one of those imaginary rewrites would have been better than what he had turned in.

Thursday morning, he dressed quickly and caught the bus to school. He hadn't told anyone what he'd tried to do. He had intentionally hidden it, so that if nothing happened he wouldn't be embarrassed. But he slowly realized that school had become his home base, in a way, the only place he allowed himself to dream. If he was going to be embarrassed because he took a giant step and fell, school should be the place. Here he was among friends who could comfort him, tell him he had done a good thing in trying, even if it hadn't worked out.

This line of reasoning led him to place a call from school to Mr. Baldwin that afternoon. He dialed the number and closed his eyes. A male voice answered so quickly it startled him.

"Baldwin."

Roundhead paused. "Uh, Mr. Baldwin. Hello, sir. I was just calling because I hadn't heard — "

Mr. Baldwin interrupted. "Yeah! Where you been? I been looking around for your phone number and didn't have it. Your story's in the paper today."

"It is?"

"Look, I wanna talk to you. Can you get over here this afternoon?"

Roundhead hung up the receiver and hugged himself as he leaned against the phone. Then he saw that it was 3:40. If he sprinted he could catch the number 10 bus, which would take him up the hill and leave him not far from the office. He tore out of the door past the pep rally in progress through the circle of school buses that took the students home. His book bag seemed heavier now that he had to run with it, and by the time he was halfway to the bus stop, he saw the driver closing the door. Roundhead speeded up, calling out, "Hey—hey! Wait up, bus driver!" The driver saw him, stopped, and let him on. He jerked his thumb behind him, saying, "There's another one coming right behind me." Roundhead didn't care. This was *his* bus, *his* time, and he knew it.

At the office, Mr. Baldwin actually got out of his chair when Roundhead came through the door. "I thought you were dead or something," he said.

"No, sir. Just at school."

"You didn't leave me your home number. That was a great piece of work you did on the basketball game. Where did you learn to write like that?"

Roundhead shrugged and said, "I read."

"Have you seen the story?" Roundhead shook his head. Mr. Baldwin escorted him to the back and opened the newspaper. There he saw his article in black and white. He felt dizzy with excitement. His name was at the top of the story, in bold type.

"Can I have a copy to show my parents?" Roundhead asked.

"Sure, you can have as many as you like—within reason." Mr. Baldwin sat down, removed a piece of paper from his desk, and scrawled his signature to it. "This is for you."

Roundhead picked up the piece of paper and saw that it

was a check for twenty-five dollars made out to him. Mr. Baldwin leaned back into his chair. "So, how does it feel to get your first story published?"

"I still can't believe it," Roundhead said.

"Look," said Mr. Baldwin, "I'm always interested in talented Negro writers, and you're one of them, despite your age. You conduct yourself very well, have good manners. I think you could do well in this business." He paused to look at Roundhead, who was still staring at the check in disbelief. Twenty-five dollars for one story. He could do so much with that money: buy his own books, go to movies, give his sisters, who weren't allowed to work, a little money for themselves.

He was thinking all of this and not listening to Mr. Baldwin, who said, "What I mean is, I'd like you to be on permanent assignment for us covering high school football and basketball. That means on Thursday and Friday nights, you'll have to make the rounds to the different schools to get the stories. I don't expect you to get them all, of course. But I want you to cover Taft, Withrow, Hughes—the big teams as far as our community is concerned. Then you write it up and bring it to me. And I'll pay you twenty-five dollars a week, plus expenses. How's that sound?"

"On assignment?" Roundhead asked. "You mean—permanent? Writing for *you*?"

Mr. Baldwin nodded. "Yeah—if that's all right," he said sarcastically as he reached out to shake Roundhead's hand. The boy stumbled forward awkwardly, took that long slender hand, and held on to it for dear life.

"Thank you, Mr. Baldwin. Thank you so much. Thank you," he kept saying, unable to let go of Mr. Baldwin's hand. "I'll do the best job anybody's ever done for you."

Mr. Baldwin managed to get his hand back and smiled at Roundhead. "I don't doubt it," he said.

When Roundhead left the office, snow had begun to fall and the temperature had dropped precipitously. He had heard it would be a long cold winter. But as he set off into the wind, he was looking up and thanking God that He had spared him long enough to see this day.

.

Afterword

Mother continued her private studies at the dinner table and became a burn specialist at Shriner's Institute, increasing her salary and security. She raised six children while advancing in her career and went on to become a great creator of motivational aphorisms like "Ain't fell in a bucket of paint" and "Can't do won't do."

Father received a certificate in boiler room operations and later became the head steam engineer at several schools. Shortly after his certification, he sold the family's six-thousand-dollar, six-room house and moved to what seemed like a mansion in fashionable North Avondale. He had forever pulled himself and his family out of poverty and debt. He retired at age fifty-five.

Grandmama continued to own several pieces of property in the city, where she struggled, like her mother before her, to keep it out of the hands of city officials who wanted to condemn it. She maintained her wonderful wit and warmth until she died of liver cancer at the age of sixty-seven.

Mr. Gene lived to be at least 100 years old and continued to regale the family with lies, old wives' tales, and half-truths. After Grandmama died, he lived with Mother and Father until they could no longer care for him, after which they placed him in a nursing home. In 1989 Mr. Gene was found walking aimlessly toward the Kentucky border. When the police asked him where he was headed, he said, "Home." He died shortly thereafter.

Picklehead, who was always much smarter than Roundhead, forgave her brother for his many dirty tricks and sailed through Auburn Hills High School with nearly perfect grades. She went on to attend Simmons College in Boston.

Little Roundhead wrote many stories for Mr. Baldwin and earned more than five hundred dollars for all of them over a period of years. By the time he was sixteen, he had established himself as a working journalist and had a portfolio that allowed him to segue into writing occasional editorials for the *Cincinnati Enquirer.* At sixteen, he became the assistant director of publicity for the city of Cincinnati's summer youth program; he held the job for two consecutive years, and it helped finance his college education.

Playwright, journalist, and corporate consultant, Syl Jones has been writing professionally since the age of 14. A native of Cincinnati, Ohio, Jones confronted controversial physicist William B. Shockley concerning heredity and race in a memorable interview published in *Playboy* magazine in 1980. Since then, he has been named a National Endowment for the Arts Playwrighting Fellow and is the only playwright to have won both the Cornerstone Prize and the Mixed Blood Versus American national playwrighting competitions. His plays have also been honored by the McKnight, Jerome, Dayton Hudson, and General Mills foundations. He has been a corporate executive at Control Data, General Mills, and Medtronic, and continues to provide consulting services to a number of companies in the Twin Cities area of Minnesota. Jones, 44, writes a regular column for the *Minneapolis Star Tribune* and lives with his wife, Cindy, in Excelsior, Minnesota.

Interior design by Will Powers.
Typeset in ITC Giovanni
by Stanton Publication Services, Inc.
Printed on acid-free Liberty paper by Quebecor Printing.